Grow to Eat

A Practical Guide to Growing Colourful and Delicious Veg from Seed

Rob Smith
@robsallotment

Photography by Sam Folan

Hardie Grant

QUADRILLE

Contents

Introduction

For those of us who love to grow our own food, there really is no better feeling than harvesting fresh veggies and knowing how they were grown, where they were grown and what they were grown in. That said, the best feeling of all must be when you make your way back to the kitchen with an armful of home-grown goodies with the anticipation of what you are going to do with them – eat them fresh, freeze for later or pickle to preserve – after all, we Grow to Eat!

I've been growing my own food for as long as I can remember. It all started with my grandad in his big allotment, where I was amazed by the fact that a small seed that looked like a tiny stone could grow into something as colourful and delicious as the vegetables we harvested later in the year. From running around the garden with a net to keep butterflies away – resulting in me smashing all the onions to the ground (sorry, Grandad) – to helping move an old dolly tub full of rainwater and putting my foot through the rusted patch, I've learnt from experience and I've loved every minute of it!

As an enthusiastic ten-year-old I persuaded my mum to give me the responsibility of a small one-metre square patch of our garden, where I spent hours sowing, thinning and harvesting my own food. This resulted in almost every meal containing radishes of some sort – after all, they are perfect to keep a kid's interest in the garden as they grow so quickly.

When I went to university I only had a kitchen windowsill to grow on, resulting in my love for chillies and herbs, the perfect flavour-packed plants for small spaces. Next came my first flat, with a balcony, and my pride and joy there were a pyramid bay tree and a hanging basket of tomatoes. If you came over, there was always the distinct aroma of bay, with its sweet spiciness coming from the kitchen – I used it in everything from cauliflower cheese to curries and soups – and the tomatoes were eaten quicker than they could grow! My next flat had no outside space at all, but my desire to grow my own food became unbearable, resulting in my becoming the custodian of my first allotment. It may have been an overgrown patch of ground that had never been loved or used at all, but with dogged determination, several broken spades, many cups of tea made on a camp stove and help from family and friends, I managed to create a productive, if somewhat ramshackle, growing space that I loved.

Fast-forward several years, and I finally moved my allotment garden to my home, creating a modern kitchen garden with raised beds where I love to experiment, grow new things and produce the tastiest, most colourful food I can, all while documenting my progress and sharing my experiences on social media (@RobsAllotment).

As my garden developed, so did my work life, and now I write for multiple national gardening magazines and work with several gardening companies to develop and launch new vegetable seeds and plants into the UK and beyond, allowing every gardener to share my love for growing their own delicious, home-grown food with ease.

Why Grow Your Own?

There is an inbuilt need in some of us to grow our own food; be it on a windowsill, in a raised bed in the garden or on a fully fledged allotment – we can't help but want to grow!

This unstoppable force comes from one place... our tummies. After all, we eat what we grow, and we grow to eat!

By growing our own food, we are aware of how it is produced, meaning we know it's healthy and chemical-free, as we've seen it from seed to harvest. Fresh vegetables are good for us, and we're told this by many different sources on an almost daily basis, yet the selection available in shops and supermarkets is a fraction of the varieties that are on offer to us to grow at home. From orange beetroots and black carrots to blue tomatoes and yellow beans, growing your own food allows you to tap into a treasure trove of different vegetables and varieties.

Sustainability and reducing your carbon footprint are also important factors to consider when deciding to grow your own food; it's more friendly to the planet if you grow your own asparagus in the back garden, rather than buy spears that have been grown in Kenya, wrapped in plastic and transported around the globe to your nearest supermarket.

I honestly think it's a life skill to know how to grow, prepare and cook your own food. Being able to spend time outside, away from electronic devices, hands in the soil, soaking up the knowledge of gardening family and friends, or simply having time to decompress and get away from daily life: there is no better way to relax. In fact, in some parts of the UK doctors are even prescribing 'gardening' as a medicine to combat anxiety and depression.

Alongside all the benefits of knowing where your food comes from, how it's grown and all the exciting new varieties on offer, you also get the physical benefits of working your plot. From digging and planting to carrying compost and pushing wheelbarrows around, it all adds up to a fantastic workout without the need for gym membership!

So, with all this in mind, there really has never been a better time to start growing your own food.

When it comes to where you will be growing your vegetables, size doesn't necessarily matter. Regardless of whether you have a windowsill, balcony, garden or allotment, you can make the most of your growing space, and I'll help you to do that.

Before you get started, there are four important questions to consider to help you choose what to grow.

Will I eat it? There are so many gardeners who grow particular veg because they've read they should be growing them, or everyone they know grows them, but in fact they themselves don't eat them. What's the point in spending all that effort, time, money and space on something you won't eat? It's far better to grow what you know you will enjoy, even if it means you only grow a few types of vegetable. You may not eat them all fresh, but if you have a surplus there are multiple ways to preserve and store almost any veg – from pickling, jamming, freezing fresh, drying and simply making your favourite dish and freezing it for a taste of summer later in the year. We grow to eat, so only grow what you know you'll eat!

Have I got space for it? Think clever; every gardener has fallen into the trap of seeing an amazing type of vegetable that they simply have to try growing, yet never thinking about how much space it would take up. We've all done it; it's part of being passionate about growing. However, when you're looking at what you want to grow and making a list of all the varieties you'd love to try, add the size at the side and it will save you a lot of heartache. Cramming more veg into your plot may be tempting, but if you have too many plants, you can easily create conditions where they shade each other, don't get the water and space they need, and where pests will thrive.

Have I chosen the right-sized plant – where I want to grow it? For example, tomatoes don't all have to be grown as cordons in a greenhouse. Instead, choose smaller bush varieties that can be grown in pots, or opt for blight-resistant ones that will crop outside without the need for the warmth of a greenhouse.

Think skyward! Not just climbing plants, but those grown in hanging baskets that take no ground space at all; it's a great way to grow tomatoes and some cucumbers. Some varieties of plant will be taller than others or will climb, meaning they use a smaller footprint of ground and produce their crops vertically. You don't need to use half your space just to get a decent crop of peas – simply avoid the shorter, more readily available varieties and choose one of the climbing ones instead. By doing this you will only use a small amount of space and they'll produce lots of pods on tall, 2m (6½ft) high plants. The same goes for squashes and courgettes, which can produce large, bushy plants, yet growing a trailing type allows you to train them up arches, fences or wires screwed into a wall. In fact, you can even train them up and along old pallets on the allotment.

◄ Lettuce seedling

Where to Grow, What to Grow, How to Grow!

Can I buy it cheaper in the shops? Let me be blunt: unless you have a large allotment or lots of space, why would you grow bog-standard brown onions or potatoes that you can buy in the shops for pennies? Yes, I know they taste better when they are home-grown and you are reassured because you know how they were grown, but you must think 'was it worth it?' If the answer is yes, that's great, keep growing what you want. However, if you're happy to buy brown onions and large white potatoes from the shops, this opens up a whole new world for that space. You can still grow potatoes, but why not try one of the coloured varieties instead? Not only do they have skins in every colour from burgundy to purple, the flesh on some of them is also coloured and results in the most amazing chips, wedges, roasties and mash. Calling it unicorn mash gets the kids asking for more every time, trust me!

Instead of basic brown onions, how about trying sweeter, pink-fleshed ones, which are delicious cooked or raw in salads. There's even one called 'Walla Walla' that's so sweet you can eat it like an apple (see page 90), although I prefer it in salads as it won't have your eyes watering while you chop it.

What about carrots? How about swapping your standard orange ones for rainbow mixes of yellow, white, red, pink and purple? They taste just the same as their more standard cousins yet cost a fortune in the shops, and they look amazing when cooked because they keep their colour. Having a plate full of these chopped into sticks on a cheeseboard or with a pot of hummus when friends come over really has the 'wow' factor.

Even if you have all the space in the world, why not grow something different that you can't buy? If you love tomatoes, why grow 'Gardener's Delight' every year when there are some amazing-looking and deliciously tasty alternatives out there. You can get speckled, striped, blue, green and even black varieties that you'll never see in a shop. It really is worth swapping one plant and trying something different that you can't buy!

If you want to harvest more veg from the same space, why not grow plants together? There are certain plants that will happily grow together, and some that even benefit from the situation. Growing basil under your tomato plants will save space, giving you two crops from the one bed, and the basil will also help keep whitefly and other critters off your tomatoes. This type of companion planting can produce more veg from the same space, which is perfect if you don't have much room to begin with. Carrots and spring onions are another beneficial couple, with the pungent onions deterring carrot fly and helping to keep your roots in tip-top condition.

There are also plants you can grow together that don't benefit each other, but they will double your harvest, which is a technique known as intercropping. Sowing a line of radishes or salad leaves in between your newly planted cabbage, cauliflower or kale plants will allow the faster-growing vegetables to be harvested before the larger, slower-growing brassicas shade them out. Again, you get more veg from the same space, so think clever when deciding what to grow, and not only will you make your gardening so much more rewarding and enjoyable, but you'll have more success.

When it comes down to how you start your vegetable plants, there are several methods to choose from.

Seed

Starting from seed gives you the widest selection of varieties and vegetables to grow, from root veg to peas, beans, tomatoes, cucumbers and more. It's also one of the most economical ways to start, as the seeds normally cost less than plants and you can start multiple seedlings for the price of one plant.

Depending on what you decide to grow, you will need some basic equipment to start from seed, including trays, pots, compost, propagators and labels. However, this is also the most time-consuming way to grow your plants as you are responsible for getting them going. Seed packets will give you all the instructions you need on how to get the best plants from your seed, but don't get too concerned with sowing depths, if it states 13mm (½ inch) and you sow it 10mm (½ inch) or 15mm (¾ inch) it really won't matter. So you can put the tape measure away. When the packet shows sowing times, these are averages across the whole country, which means if it states 'Sow in spring', you can probably sow at the beginnings of the time span if you are in a warmer part of the country, while those in cooler areas are better to wait a little later for it to warm up.

▶ Beetroot seeds

Seedlings or plug plants

These are young plants that have only just got their 'true' seed leaves – those that follow the very first ones. Normally despatched by online and mail-order companies, they will be delivered through your letterbox and will need potting up and growing on before they can be planted in the greenhouse or garden. Plug plants are an economical way to fill your garden with plants, but, there is a limited supply of varieties available compared to seed. So hunt around and check all the suppliers, as they will all have some different varieties. You will need to transplant your plug plants into larger pots and grow them on before they can be planted, but they will be delivered to you at the correct time of year to allow for this, and within weeks they'll be in the ground.

Potted plants

These are the typical plants you find in the garden centre, usually starting in 9cm (3½in) pots, or trays of six large modules, then increasing in size. These are ideal for those gardeners who have less time to start their plants off at home. These plants will only require you to keep them inside until the last frost has passed, then they will be happy in the garden and won't need potting on beforehand. Your selection of available varieties will be smaller than of seeds or plug plants, but it will normally include all the favourites and a couple of new ones each year. Potted plants are a great way to start growing your own if you aren't sure about how to start seeds, or don't have the time, equipment or space to do so.

Bare roots, bulbs, cloves, slips and tubers

This covers everything other than seeds and plants in compost, including seed potatoes, onion sets and garlic cloves. Most of these can be planted straight outside into the garden or in containers, making them easy to grow and good for beginners and experienced gardeners alike. Bare-root vegetables are plants that have been dug from a field and had the soil removed before being sold while dormant for planting, in winter. This category also includes rhubarb and asparagus, which are known as crowns. Slips are the rooted cuttings of sweet potatoes and will need potting up to produce plants before they are transplanted into their growing space.

Grafted plants

These are plants that have a different rootstock to their own. They are produced by taking the super-charged roots from one plant and adding to those the tasty top plant you want to harvest from. There is nothing genetically modified about these plants; they are created using the same methods used to produce grafted fruit trees or roses.

Whereas fruit trees are grafted by adding a certain type of rootstock to determine the overall vigour and height of the tree, grafted vegetables are created to crop up to 75 per cent more per plant and to crop earlier than if they were grown from seed alone. Originally created for the commercial growers who produce fruit for supermarkets, this method of producing plants has now been introduced into the domestic market for gardeners to grow at home. Grafted plants are more expensive than those grown from one seed, as it takes up to seven people to create one grafted plant. Therefore, these plants are only available for a few weeks each spring and are highly sought-after, selling out quickly. The number of varieties available as grafted plants is limited, but they are well worth growing, especially if you don't have much space, as you get so much more fruit per plant.

▶ Grafted aubergine plant

You can grow your own food just about anywhere and in any container that will hold compost. From open fields and garden borders to allotment sites and concrete yards, I've seen carrots growing in old welly boots, beetroots in wheelbarrows and lettuce in old guttering. Therefore, even if you have no open ground to grow in, you can still produce plenty of home-grown veg.

Growing in the ground

This is perhaps the most popular and easiest way to grow your own vegetables, with most allotment holders and back-garden growers using this method. Growing directly in the soil allows you to grow just about any vegetable you want, as long as your soil suits the plant. It's well worth using a soil-testing kit to see what type of soil you have, as this will determine what will grow well there. For example, blueberries love acidic soil, whereas cabbages prefer alkaline, so growing them in the opposite soils will lead to disappointment and failure. That said, you can alter the acidity of your soil by adding garden lime to make it more alkaline, or by adding ericaceous compost to create a more acidic area. However, I find it best to grow what is suited to your soil rather than planting something in a container of what suits them better as the only option. The downside to growing directly into the earth is that you are always bending over to do anything, so it can put a strain on your back.

Adding compost and other organic matter to your soil will benefit your plants, as they contribute nutrients that are required by your plants to perform at their best.

Manure

Most people will be familiar with adding this soil improver to garden beds, whether cow, horse, chicken or 'farmyard' manure, which is usually a mix of cow and horse manures. Hungry plants, such as squash, beans and brassicas (cabbage-type plants) will thank you for the added feed, producing bigger plants and better harvests. So will root crops like carrots and parsnips. However, you must add the manure to the bed the autumn before you grow the plants, because fresh manure can cause the roots to fork, warp or become stunted.

Green manure

Nothing to do with animals, green manure is when you grow plants such as rye, clover or phacelia in your beds in autumn, then chop them down and dig them in the following spring. By doing this you can add lots of nutrients to your soil without needing to carry heavy loads of animal manure around the garden. There are certain types for different jobs; some will improve the soil structure with their roots, while others will add nitrogen by fixing it from the atmosphere and storing it in their roots. This means the next vegetable to grow in that space will have access to that nitrogen as a free feed.

You will find more on green manures online, plus which plants are best grown after different green manures to make the most of your soil.

Compost

Compost dug into the soil makes it more workable and adds goodness; it's especially beneficial for clay soils as they are sticky and can be difficult to grow in when they become wet. By adding compost, and either digging it in or leaving it on the soil surface to let worms work it down through the earth, you help prevent the soil forming large 'clods'. At the other end of the spectrum, adding compost to very free-draining, sandy soils will increase the amount of water the soil can hold and prevent it drying out so quickly in hotter or windier weather.

Either way, adding compost to your garden beds or allotment plots is always a good thing, and well worth the effort. If you are using homemade compost, make sure you break up any larger chunks and remove the odd bits of sticky tape or plastic that always seem to make their way into it (even when you remove it from cardboard and paper before composting). Shop-bought compost can be added, but it can be very expensive if you need lots of it, so consider buying a large dumpy bag, or ask local suppliers to deliver it by the van load if you can. Always use peat-free compost, as this is better for the environment – there are plenty of suppliers now.

Leaf mould

It may sound strange, but leaf mould is a great addition to your garden. Basically, it is created by letting leaves break down into a fine, crumbly, compost-like substance. You collect the leaves in autumn, stuff them in old compost bags, then make some holes in the bottom, seal the top and leave the bag somewhere for a year or so to break down. During the summer you may need to open the bag and water the contents to make sure they are damp, as this helps speed up the composting process. What you are left with after a year (or more, depending on the type of leaf), can be added to your garden as you would compost. This is the perfect way to use up leaves from any trees in and around your garden. You can also make leaf mould by creating a cage out of chicken wire propped up with stakes, then filling it with leaves and covering it to prevent the leaves blowing out. This method can be used when there is a large amount of leaves available.

For those of you with cherry trees in the garden, or nearby, you can make 'blossom mould' in the same way and add that to your garden. However, blossoms contain more water than leaves, so they will compost down a lot quicker and can be added to the garden later in the same year.

Other additions

You can add almost any organic matter you can get your hands on to your garden beds. Spent hops are something I have used before, and they are readily available from any microbrewery you may have in the area – mine bags them up after brewing and leaves them for the local allotmenteers to help themselves to. There isn't really any nutritional benefit to adding hops, but it will help to lighten the soil and improve its structure.

Mushroom compost can also be added, which is the compost used to grow mushroom crops commercially. However, make sure it's not a peat-based compost, as this is bad for the environment, plus it will increase the acidity of your plot. Again, it doesn't have that much goodness in it, but adding any organic matter will improve soil structure.

Raised beds

I'll hold my hands up and say I'm biased here, as most of my growing space is made up of raised beds! When I created my kitchen garden, I had to transform a sloping field into a growing space I could enjoy and that would be productive, which meant we needed to create tiers. As the garden started to take shape, I knew I wanted it to look as attractive as possible and found that raised beds not only add structure and interest during the winter months, but they are also more manageable for weeding, as you can set your sights on one bed at a time, giving yourself achievable goals without over-reaching yourself.

Raised bed gardening allows you to create the perfect soil substrate for any plant you want to grow, so it's no issue if you want to grow acid-loving blueberries in one bed, while the one next to it has alkaline-liking cauliflowers. That said, this potential benefit is also the biggest problem with raised beds, especially when you have a lot of them, as you need to fill them with soil – and that can be expensive! The way I looked at this issue was by trying to emulate the rest of the garden, and therefore I used topsoil. You can buy good-quality topsoil by the tonne quite cheaply compared to compost, and because it's the same stuff you'll find in any garden border, it's just like growing in the ground. I added a majority of topsoil to my raised beds, then a thin layer of grit for drainage and a 10cm (4in) layer of manure as well. This was all mixed in and allowed to settle before being topped up; you'll be surprised how much a

raised bed will sink when it starts to settle. My metal raised beds stand on a layer of pebbles to keep the metal from sitting on the soil, prolonging the life of the beds by preventing them from rusting. The beds also have open bases, so the roots of the plants can work their way into the ground below, while I save my back from not having to bend as much. I would say that if you want to grow in metal raised beds, go for the best quality you can afford, as some are so thin you can put your garden fork through them, and they easily bend.

Pots, troughs and other containers

Most of us are familiar with growing in these, and there are hundreds of designs and shapes available. You probably have some in your garden, but did you know you can grow plenty of vegetables in them? Galvanised cattle water troughs make excellent containers for growing root crops and potatoes. Smaller containers work well for lettuce, rocket and leafy veg, while old buckets are great for carrots and beetroot – in fact, even wheelbarrows can make perfect mini veg patches and can be moved around the garden as required. When growing in containers it's important to make sure there are drainage holes in the bottom, and that you water your plants adequately, as the smaller the container, the quicker it will dry out. You'll also need to add liquid feed to the water to make sure the plants have all the nutrients they need to perform at their best.

Sowing seed

When deciding to sow seeds, you can direct sow, which means you put the seeds directly into the soil, be it in the ground or in a raised bed/large container, or you can start your seeds off in trays, modules or any number of ways. Some of my favourite methods for sowing seed include recycling and upcycling different household items to make sowing trays/pots.

One of the easiest things to use for seed sowing must be old yoghurt or cream pots, which are about the same shape as small plant pots and need a few holes punching in the base to make them ready to use.

Larger tin cans work well for small bush tomatoes, especially if you have a restaurant or café nearby that will let you have the commercial-sized ones with tomatoes etched into the can, as they look great in the garden.

Wooden crates and those you buy satsumas in can be used to start seed in – simply line them with a double layer of newspaper and fill it with compost.

Eggshells can be used as plantable modules. Start them off in the eggbox, and plant them out shell and all. By using this method you also add a little calcium to the soil – just remember to squeeze the shell and crack it before planting, as this makes it easier for the seedlings' roots to grow through into the soil.

Lengths of old guttering can be used to start pea seeds in. All you need to do when it is time to transplant them is slide out the seeds and compost from the gutter into a pre-dug channel, and they'll romp away.

For seedlings that require a deeper root space, such as peas and beans, you can fill old toilet roll tubes with compost and use those. Simply squash them flat to create a crease down two sides, then move them a quarter turn and squash them flat again, which gives four creases and allows you to pop them open to form a square tube rather than a circular one. By doing this you can push lots of the square tubes together, fill them with compost and sow into them as it they were modules. Water the seeds sparingly or the cardboard will start to go green, and when it comes to planting-out time you can just transplant the entire thing, tube and all, into the soil.

Make the most of your space, permanently

By giving space to perennial vegetables, which are plants that come back each year, you may be sacrificing a bed permanently, but you'll be growing some of the most expensive vegetables you can buy, including asparagus, rhubarb, artichokes, perennial kale and leeks (yes, there is such a thing as a perennial leek, more on these later). With some vegetables, such as asparagus, growing for 20 years, if you have the space you'll be rewarded with fantastically fresh, home-grown spears each spring/summer. Just think how much that will save you at supermarket prices!

▶ Container-grown carrots

Root Vegetables

Root vegetables are the unsung heroes of the vegetable garden; they are able to grow in small spaces, producing heavy yields of incredibly tasty and nutritious roots and tubers, and some are among the most colourful veg you can grow.

One of the great things about root veg is their ability to store for months on end without refrigeration, meaning you can feed yourself and your family from one set of plants you've grown through the summer, unlike many other vegetables which have a short shelf-life and need eating or making into something within a few days of harvest.

When it comes to growing root vegetables you need to decide how much space you can give over to the plants. Some, such as potatoes, are relatively inexpensive to buy, so why use all your space for growing them unless there is something different about them?

Growing in the open garden, raised beds, containers and even bags, root veg are pretty versatile and easy to grow as long as you keep them well watered and weed-free. There's nothing like sticking your hand in a bucket of soil and tickling around for the first new potato of the season, or pulling your first mini carrot and munching it in the garden as you work – the flavours are simply delicious.

There are also speedy radishes, alien-looking kohl rabi and, the pickler's favourite, beetroot, along with winter staples such as celeriac and parsnips – all are easy to grow and can be stored for months.

Potatoes

Perhaps the most popular root vegetable in the country. Every allotment seems to have rows of potato plants gracing each plot, providing spuds to eat fresh or store through winter. That said, you don't need acres of space to grow potatoes, as they even grow in old buckets or compost bags filled with soil. The key is to grow what you will use and what you have the space for. So, if you only like small new potatoes for salads and have a small plot, you can grow a few earlies in buckets; whereas if you eat lots of jacket potatoes and have an allotment or larger veg garden, you can grow rows of maincrop varieties.

There are many varieties of potato, with all of them fitting under three general headings: first earlies, second earlies and maincrop. There are two extra categories, salad and Christmas potatoes (second cropping), which come from within the first three classifications and denote what the variety can be used for. This may sound complicated, but it's simply a way of explaining what the different varieties are used for and when they should be planted and harvested (roughly). For example, a salad potato can come from within any category; it will always have a waxy, buttery texture that holds together well when cooked, making it excellent to serve with a salad; plus, salad potatoes are usually harvested smaller to serve with the skin still on.

Unless you have lots of growing space and love potatoes, why not grow one of the increasing numbers of new and different potatoes? Including those with purple or blue skins, those that cook a third quicker than regular potatoes, or one of the coloured-flesh varieties that will give you pink or blue mash!

When it comes to planting and harvest times, as a rule there are four planting periods:

· First earlies are normally planted in early spring and are ready to lift in early to mid-summer.

· Second earlies are planted in mid-spring and lifted in mid-summer.

· Maincrops are planted mid- to late spring and lifted in late summer to early autumn.

· Christmas potatoes (for the UK) are planted in August (late summer) and will be ready to harvest from October (mid-autumn).

How to grow

Potatoes are grown from special seed potatoes, which are virus-free tubers. These tubers are planted in the garden or in containers, to grow into a plant, which in turn will produce a crop of edible potato tubers. Depending on the variety you choose and where you grow it, one seed potato can yield a couple of kilos (4½ pounds) of potatoes when harvested.

Potatoes are traditionally grown in the ground, especially if you are growing a lot of plants to see you through the winter. It's best to enrich the bed with compost or manure the autumn before planting your tubers, as this will ensure your plants have enough feed to produce a good crop.

The next decision is whether to chit your tubers or not. Chitting is the process of allowing your tubers to produce stout little shoots before planting; these aren't like the shoots you get on potatoes if you leave them in a cupboard too long, as chitting is done by leaving the potato in a light, frost-free place. I usually stand my potatoes up in old eggboxes or trays, with the 'eyes' (the little sprouts) pointing upwards, as this is where the shoots come from. There are arguments for and against chitting, with some saying there is no point as farmers don't complete this process, so why should a home gardener? To be honest, I only chit my tubers because I don't want them to sprout in the nylon bags they are sold in, as this can cause the shoots to be damaged or ripped off, so I stand them in trays. If you have chitted your potatoes, when it comes to planting time make sure to rub off all but four of the shoots, as this will give you larger potatoes.

Whether you chit or not, all potato tubers are grown the same way – either in rows in the ground or in pots and bags.

When growing in the ground make sure to grow your plants in a sunny spot, then dig a trench around 15cm (6in) deep, and for earlies and second earlies place your potatoes 30cm (12in) apart, with rows 60cm (24in) apart. For maincrops, the tubers should be 40cm (16in) apart and the rows wider, at 75cm (2½ft) apart. This is because maincrops usually produce larger plants and the resulting potato tubers are harvested later and larger.

As the plants begin to grow you will need to earth them up to protect early shoots from the frost and stop any developing potatoes from going green, which can make them harmful to eat. This is done by dragging soil from in between the rows and piling it up where the plants are growing, covering any foliage as it grows. This should be done a few times until there is no more chance of frost and the ridges are around 25–30cm (10–12in) tall. If you are growing in containers, the same principle applies, however, you will just start with only 10cm (4in) of compost in the bottom, add your potato tubers, and then cover with another 10cm (4in) of compost, then fill your container with a little more compost/soil as the plants grow, until the container is full, and then leave your plants to grow. When I complete my final earthing up, I like to add a sprinkle of dried chicken manure pellets, as this nitrogen-rich feed will improve the plants and their yield. Potatoes also benefit from being kept moist, so watering is critical for ensuring you get the most from your plants, especially if you are growing in containers, which dry out quicker.

Harvesting and storing

When it comes to harvesting, I like to use the tickling method to make sure my potatoes are ready. With your hand, gently work your way towards the base of the plants, 'tickling' as you go to move the soil. You will eventually find your tubers and will be able to feel how large they are. You can then harvest a couple early, if you like, while leaving the plants in situ to keep swelling the remaining tubers. Earlies want to be the size of an egg ideally, then they can be harvested and used straight away – the skin will be paper thin, easily rubbed off with your fingers or a vegetable brush. Second earlies will be a little larger, and maincrop will be the biggest. When harvesting maincrops for storage you want the tubers to have a firm, thick skin so they store for longer without going soft, which is usually done by removing the top growth of the plant. By removing the leaves you allow the plant to concentrate on drawing energy into the tubers and to thicken the skin of the potatoes. Leave them in the ground for 10–14 days to cure, before digging them up and leaving them on the surface for a few hours to allow the soil to dry. You can then brush this off and store your dry potatoes in sacks in a dark, cool, frost-free place.

For container-grown potatoes, you can simply upend your container into a wheelbarrow or onto an empty bed, then pick out all the tubers with ease. I always grow in containers rather than the open ground, as then most of my potatoes will be perfect and damage free, while those grown in the ground can suffer from slug damage and have holes in them, which means they won't store.

Top Tips

- Consider starting some first earlies or salad potatoes in containers in the greenhouse or a polytunnel. You can start them in midwinter and harvest from early summer. Simply make sure you cover the pot and plant with a double layer of horticultural fleece at night or if frost is forecast.

- If you are growing in containers, it's best to drill drainage holes around 3–5cm (1¼–2in) up the sides rather than in the base as this creates a small reservoir that the plants will appreciate in the warmer months. Potatoes like lots of water.

- Try to water your plants at the base and with rainwater, if possible. This can help prevent scab affecting your plants. Scab (see page 29) is more prevalent in alkaline soil, so adding a handful of ericaceous soil to your planting hole can also help prevent the problem.

- If you suffer from potato blight in your area, consider growing early potatoes, which will be harvested before your plants become infected. You can also grow your plants under a lean-to or other structure that stops rain splashing onto the foliage, as this spreads the disease.

◀ Top left: chitted potato; Top right: removing extra chitted sprouts; Centre left: planting potatoes in containers; Centre right: earting up potatoes; Bottom right: harvesting; Bottom left: 'tickling' potatoes to see their size

Christmas potatoes

These are varieties for the northern hemisphere that have been kept in cold storage until mid-summer, allowing you to plant them later. You can buy specialist tubers for this, normally called 'Christmas' or 'second cropping' potatoes, or you can keep a couple of your seed potatoes in the fridge until August and grow those. The best way to grow potatoes for Christmas is in containers, as you can move them under cover if an early frost is predicted. I grow mine in large containers, starting them in the same way as any potted potato. When the first frost is forecast, I move the pots into the unheated greenhouse, and as soon as the leaves start to yellow, I remove them all at ground level and stop watering the pots. After a week or two I move the pots into the shed, but any frost-free place will do, then leave them as they are, harvesting as many potatoes as I want by digging them out of the soil as required. By doing this you can easily harvest small 'new potatoes' on Christmas Day and beyond.

Potatoes to grow

'Heidi Red' (maincrop) – This German potato not only has a deep red skin, but the internal flesh is also bright red. This potato is great for salads and boiling as it has a buttery flesh, meaning it won't dissolve in the water when it's boiled. This variety is a great one for encouraging kids to eat their veggies, as it also makes nice crisps when thinly sliced and fried, or why not use it in potato salad?

'Purple Majesty' (maincrop) – As the name suggests, this potato has dark purple skin and internal flesh. High in anthocyanins (antioxidants), this potato is good for roasting, mashing and baking due to its high dry-matter content, meaning it's got more of a floury texture. Try mashing and serving to kids as 'unicorn mash', as they love the colour, and it also makes unusual-looking chips.

'Mayan Rose' (maincrop) – These are attractive-looking red potatoes with yellow spots and yellow flesh. Classed as a Phureja variety, 'Mayan' potatoes have the added benefit of taking a third less time to boil, making them energy efficient as well as tasty!

'Pink Fir Apple' (maincrop) – This unusual potato has knobbly tubers that are tinged with pink, with firm white flesh, making them great for use in salads or boiling. The long, slender tubers have a distinctively nutty flavour to them, which is best enjoyed served with a knob of butter and a sprinkling of salt.

'Ratte' (second early) – This is a French classic, rarely found for sale in the shops. The white-skinned, yellow-fleshed, buttery tubers date from the mid-19th century and have a distinct chestnut flavour. Even though they have an excellent flavour they almost became extinct, until a French agronomist found the original La Ratte in 1965. Now they are loved around the world for their smaller tubers that don't disintegrate when cooked.

'Charlotte' (second early/Christmas) – This must be my 'go-to' variety for producing firm, waxy potatoes for summer and Christmas. Not only are the potatoes delicious, they also have great levels of blight resistance, perfect when you're growing a potato later in the year as the weather gets wetter.

Problems

Potato blight is caused by a fungus-like organism that spreads quickly in warmer, wetter weather. You will notice small, light green/yellow patches start to develop on the leaves, followed by brown patches on the stems as the plants begin to collapse. The whole process can happen in under 48 hours, and the problem will spread throughout your plants unless measures are taken. There is no way to stop blight, but you can lessen the effects by picking off affected leaves or chopping severely affected plants to the ground; make sure to burn or dispose of affected plants in household waste bins – don't compost them. Any fallen leaves should be collected and disposed of, and you should grow your plants in a different bed the following year. Tubers from blighted plants are perfectly edible, but should be eaten quickly, as they won't store for long. If blight is a persistent problem, you may want to grow blight-resistant varieties, such as 'Sarpo Mira' (maincrop), 'Acoustic' (second early), or 'Colleen' (first early). Potato blight can spread to tomato plants so don't grow them too close together.

'Scab' is the result of certain pathogens causing the skin on potato tubers to develop scab-like rough patches. Starting in summer, scab is more prevalent in dry soils, so it's important to water potato plants well and keep the area moist – adding organic matter such as compost or manure to the bed will help. Soil that is more alkaline can also encourage scab, so try not to grow potatoes in a bed that had cabbages or cauliflowers in it the previous year, especially if you added garden lime. You can add a few spades-full of ericaceous compost to the bed, which will make the soil less alkaline. Affected tubers may look unpleasant, however, they are perfectly edible but should have the skin peeled before consumption.

◄ 'Heidi Red (left) and 'Purple Majesty' (right)

This is a root vegetable that seems pretty humble, yet is so versatile in the kitchen. From cakes and juices to dips and casseroles, we use carrots for a vast array of dishes. We are all familiar with the typical orange carrot, seen wrapped in plastic bags in almost every supermarket in the country, yet did you know you can grow red, yellow, pink, purple, multi-coloured and even black carrots at home? In fact, carrots were never orange originally, they were white, purple or yellow! Plus they don't have to be long thin roots, you can grow some that are round like ping-pong balls, or bigger than a cricket ball. Happy in just about any space, carrots can be grown in the open ground, raised beds, pots and containers, or even window boxes if you choose the right variety for the space you have. I always start an early sowing in an old galvanised bucket that's full of holes, as it's the perfect space to grow slender, finger-sized roots.

How to grow

Carrots are one of those crops that is pretty easy to grow and care for, but you have to get the basics right to ensure success. As with all vegetables, the key is in the soil; this time you don't want overly rich, manure-laden soil, as this will cause your carrots to fork, warp and grow into crazy shapes. The ideal soil for carrots had manure added to it in the previous year but has had something growing in since then, perhaps courgettes or potatoes, as the act of harvesting your tubers will have broken up the soil, making it finer and more suited to carrots. If you are growing in the ground or a raised bed it's best to avoid heavy, clay soil as this can cause misshapen roots; ideally, you'd want to add some sand to create a more open-structured soil. If you can't do this, consider growing in containers of compost instead, or grow a rounder, fatter-shaped carrot such as 'Oxheart', as it forms half of the root above soil level, while the blunt tip is wider than most and doesn't fork, coping well with clay and stony soil.

The more traditional way of growing carrots is to form a shallow, straight drill in the soil with a trowel, cane or dibber. It wants to be around 1cm (½in) deep and subsequent rows should be 15–25cm (6–10in) apart. Next, water the drills, then sow the seeds thinly, as you don't want to disturb the seedlings because this can attract carrot fly, which can ruin your crop. After covering the seeds and labelling them, it's best to pin a piece of insect-proof netting or chicken wire over the top, which protects the seeds from birds who will flick the soil around in a recently cultivated bed. Once they get growing you can remove the netting. Carrot seed can be slow to germinate, so don't worry if it seems to be taking a couple of weeks. When the leaves of your carrots are around 2–3cm (¾–1¼in) tall you want to thin your plants to 5–8cm (2–3in) apart as this will allow for the largest roots to form.

◄ 'Carruba' F1 over-wintered in a greenhouse

Carrots

The renegade's way of sowing carrots is less precise, yet just as productive. I call it the 'Throw and Grow' method, which I discovered when I dropped a full packet's worth of seed in a bed by accident! Make sure the bed you are growing in is weed-free and has fine soil, as with the previous method, but this time just sprinkle your seeds into the bed, scattering them finely, then get a rake and lightly work the seeds into the soil before watering. This may sound crazy, but by growing like this you harvest all the roots, starting with the ones that are ready first, and effectively thinning the rest, giving them more room to grow.

If you prefer to grow in containers, it's best to sift together compost and sand, or at least work it with your hands to make sure there are no large lumps present. As with the renegade method, sprinkle seeds thinly around the entire container and cover with 1cm (½in) of compost, making sure to leave the container in full sun and keeping the compost moist. You can use this method for any variety, but if you are growing a long-rooted one, be sure to harvest them while small, before they hit the base of the container. Ideally, you want at least 30cm (12in) soil depth, so old buckets with drainage holes work well. However, if your container is shallower it's best to grow a shorter carrot that will fit.

Harvesting and storing

Carrots are easy to harvest; simply hold the leaves and lever the roots from the soil with a garden fork while firmly pulling upwards. Some varieties have more foliage than others, making harvesting easier, but if you loosen the soil with a fork, you will be fine. Don't yank or pull the leaves sharply as they will come away from the root, leaving you to dig it free and risk damaging surrounding carrots.

Most of us use carrots fresh from the garden, happily getting through the harvest as the roots are pulled. However, for those who want to store their harvest, you can lay the undamaged roots (after removing the leaves) in a box with sand, alternating the sand and carrot layers, finishing with sand on top – this will help prevent the roots shrivelling and drying up. Keep the box dry and frost-free, and you can remove and use the carrots as you need them.

- Thin your carrots on a windy day so carrot fly can't home in on where they are growing.

- To help mask the smell of carrots, you can grow spring onions between your carrot rows, or around the perimeter of the bed, to confuse the fly, meaning it can't find your carrots.

- Sow a small row or pinch of seed every two weeks to keep you in sweet roots all season. You can even sow seeds in an unheated greenhouse early or late in the year, extending your crop even further.

◄ Top left: creating a shallow drill; Top right: preparing to sow; Bottom left: thinly sowing seeds; Bottom right: labelling the row

Carrots to grow

'Yellow Moon' F1 – This sunshine-yellow variety produces 15–18cm (6–7in) roots and has a mild, sweet flavour. It is yellow all the way to the leaves, unlike some others, which produce a green shoulder. Plants have a strong, upright habit, which makes them easier to pull without the risk of snapping. Perhaps the best-tasting of the yellow carrots, particularly good served with dips.

'Black Nebula' – As the name suggests, this carrot is so dark, it almost looks black. Containing masses of anthocyanin to give it the dark purple colour, it remains dark even when cooked. When juiced the resulting drink is incredibly dark and sweet, magically turning bright pink if you add lemon juice!

'Red Sun' F1 – A bright red carrot that's sweeter than its orange counterparts due to its thick, sweet core. Keeping its colour when cooked, it's also great to snack on raw as it has that addictive sweetness.

'White Satin' F1 – An unusual, fully white carrot that looks like a parsnip at first glance! Smooth, sweet and juicy, this variety tastes every bit as good as its orange cousins, just without the colour. The roots get to around 20cm (8in) long.

'Purple Haze' F1 - A deep purple carrot that holds a surprise in store... its core is orange! This unusual carrot is certain to get cooks and gardeners alike excited, especially as it has a sweet, almost spicy flavour when eaten raw.

'Rondo' – This ping-pong-ball-shaped carrot is the ideal one to grow in shallower containers or stonier ground as it doesn't have a large root to fork or twist. Instead, it produces almost spherical carrots which are easy to harvest and are loved by kids. Ideal to harvest small and cook in orange juice with a little butter for a delicious side dish.

'Oxheart' – This old French variety is from the world-famous carrot region of Nantes. It produces 10–12cm (4–4½in) thick roots which are as long as they are wide, with a snub-nosed point, making them great for clay or stony soils as they don't grow very deep. This crisp, sweet carrot also seems to be resistant to carrot fly in my experience – perhaps this is due to the fact that each root produces surprisingly little leaf for the size of the carrot.

'Carruba' F1 – This modern variety is extremely bolt- resistant, meaning it can be sown in mid-winter in an unheated greenhouse, growing all winter and cropping before you need the space back for tomatoes. Ideally, it is best to grow in containers or troughs if you have a wet site. This carrot can also be grow outside from spring.

Problems

Carrot fly can be a pain when growing carrots, as the flies' larvae can tunnel through carrots, parsnips and parsley roots, causing damage and meaning the affected roots can't be stored, as they will rot. To avoid the problem, make sure you sow your seed sparsely, as the smell of plants being thinned can attract the adult flies. You can also cover your crop with fine-mesh insect netting, or grow a resistant variety such as 'Resistafly' F1, 'Flyaway' F1 or 'Oxheart'. Carrot flies produce multiple generations of offspring in one year, but sowing after late spring will avoid the first generation, while harvesting before late summer will miss the second.

▶ Top left: 'Yellow Moon' F1;
Top right: 'Rondo'; Bottom
left: 'Red Sun' F1; Bottom
right: 'Carruba' F1

Beetroots

Beetroots, or beets, are probably one of the first vegetables I remember growing with my grandad; he used to grow them and my grandma would pickle great batches. Not always everyone's cup of tea, pickled beetroot can sometimes be overpoweringly sour if you use malt vinegar, so try apple cider vinegar instead – it's a game-changer for pickling!

A multi-use crop, beetroot can be grown as a baby leaf for salads, mature leaves to use as spinach, or for the roots, which can be used in a whole manner of ways in the kitchen. It is mainly thought of as a dark purple, finger-staining globe that can taste earthy and strong; you really need to grow your own to appreciate this vegetable to the fullest.

There are lots of different types of beetroot available to grow in the garden, including super-sweet, bright orange, white and even striped ones, all easy to grow in the open ground or in containers. You can even harvest your beetroot at different sizes depending on what you want to use them for; smaller golf-ball-size roots are particularly tender and flavourful, whereas larger roots can be stored for winter and roasted in the oven as you would a potato. I love to roast my beetroot chopped into pieces, with a little olive oil and a glug of balsamic vinegar, which helps bring out the sweetness and makes a delicious side dish for chicken or served cold with salads. However, my favourite use for the roots is to make them into a beetroot and horseradish chutney – it's incredible and goes with salads, cheese, cooked meats and even smoked salmon.

How to grow

Beetroot is a vegetable that's nice and easy to grow. Simply create a shallow drill in weed-free, raked soil, thinly sow the seed, cover and wait for them to grow; it's that easy! As the seedlings begin to appear you want to thin them to 5cm (2in) spacings, using the thinnings in salads or sandwiches as a baby leaf, which allows you to harvest the other beetroot as they get to golf-ball-sized. By thinning your beetroots you are leaving space for the remaining plants to swell and get larger.

You can also multi-sow your plants in modules in an unheated greenhouse, which allows you to plant out seedlings where they will grow. It's a good way to grow if the place where you want your beetroot isn't ready for the plants yet, or if your plot is prone to flooding. I sow 3–4 seeds per cell, leaving them to germinate and reach 5–6cm (2–2½in) tall before planting them out as a cluster of seedlings (there's no need to separate them). As the cluster grows you can harvest the leaves and/or roots as you like, and because of the way the plants grow they will simply push against each other and produce a group of roots close together without any reduction in plant size. This is particularly attractive if you sow several colours together, as you will get a kaleidoscope cluster, which really is impressive.

When it comes to feeding beetroot, this may sound strange, but you can use salt! Not masses, and only once, but it will help your plants grow and make them taste better. Firstly, you must remember that beetroots evolved from coastal plants, which would have had salt air and water around them all the time. In fact, sugar beet are descended from the same plants and farmers use salt on them as a fertiliser. I found this

▶ Top to bottom, 'Golden Eye', 'Jolie' F1, 'Chioggia'

recommendation in an old gardening book of my grandad's, which advised adding 1 level teaspoon of salt to a 9 litre (2 gallon) watering can and watering the beetroot with this until the soil is moist (avoiding the leaves). It should only be done once in the plants' life, ideally when they are around 10cm (4in) tall. As it's such a small amount of salt, it won't hurt the soil for subsequent crops, but it will help the beetroot as it has trace minerals in it, including boron, which a lack of can cause internal black spots in beets. If you still aren't convinced, water one row with untreated water and another with one dose of salt water – you'll notice the difference. You can also feed plants with a high-nitrogen fertiliser such as sulphate of ammonia or dried chicken manure pellets if they don't seem to be growing strongly.

When it comes to watering your plants, they should be kept just moist; too dry and they can become woody, while if they are watered too much they will produce leafier tops to the detriment of swelling and producing a decent root.

Harvesting and storing

Beetroot have the reputation of staining anything they touch, especially gardeners' hands when they are removing the leaves from the roots. To mitigate this, try twisting the leaves to remove them rather than cutting them, as this dramatically reduces how much they will 'bleed' and stain your hands. Don't consign the leaves to the compost bin as they can be cooked like spinach or chard when large, and the smaller ones are great added to salads and sandwiches. If you don't eat all your beetroots fresh or preserve them, the roots can be stored in pretty much the same way as carrots, in boxes of sand in a dry, frost-free place. By doing this you'll have roots available to use 'fresh' for months.

Beetroots to grow

'Jolie' F1 – This new beetroot may be purple like many others, but what sets it apart from those is the taste; it's super-sweet and has none of the earthiness to it, meaning the flavour is just about perfect. This beetroot is great for steaming or boiling and serving cold with summer salads.

'Golden Eye' – A beautifully golden-orange beetroot with attractive rings when sliced in half. It won't stain your hands or clothes and has a deliciously sweet taste, plus the light-green leaves can be used as a veggie. I like this one roasted in the oven to intensify the sweetness.

'Albina Verduna' – An ice-white beetroot that's been around from before 1800. Again, this beet is sweeter than most purple ones, with light green, white-ribbed leaves that are delicious in their own right. As it's an older variety, don't let the roots get too large before harvesting as they can go a little woody.

'Chioggia' – The showstopper of the beetroot world! This Italian heirloom variety has gorgeous concentric circles of pink and white, giving rise to its common name, 'Candy Cane' beetroot. Cooking will cause the rings to bleed and go a lovely shade of pink, so it's best to enjoy this stunner raw in salads or as raw beetroot carpaccio with goat's cheese. Thinly sliced, tossed with a splash of oil and vinegar, this beetroot tastes as good as it looks.

'Rouge Crapaudine' – Thought to be the oldest beetroot still available, this carrot-shaped root has become massively popular again after featuring on multiple TV cooking programmes because of its renowned flavour. Famed for creating beetroot 'steaks' cooked in beef fat, this root will store incredibly well because of its thick, bark-like skin. Try cooking in beef fat on a very low heat, covered for 3–4 hours and the flavour will be meaty, smoky and sublime.

Problems

Bolting is the main problem; this is when the plant begins to produce a flower spike and stops increasing the size of the root. It's normally caused by the plant becoming stressed, or because of a lack of moisture, a sudden hot spell or sowing at the incorrect time. Try to keep the plant moist, but not too wet, and remove any plants that begin to bolt, eating the leaves and composting the plant, as the root won't swell and will be woody.

Beet leaf miners are insects that look like house flies. Their larvae tunnel into beetroot leaves, leaving tell-tale tracks, and while they won't damage the roots they can cause issues if you are growing beetroot for edible leaves. If only a few leaves are affected you can squish the larvae in the leaf, removing and composting it. Alternatively, you can cover your plants with an insect-proof netting.

◄ Top: multi-sown beetroot seedlings; Centre: coloured roots of seedlings; Bottom: transplanting multi-sown seedlings
► Beetroot, which has bolted

Perhaps the easiest and fastest-cropping vegetable you can grow at home, with some being harvested in as little as 18 days from sowing. The crunchy, spicy roots are great to snack on raw, or add to salads or slaw, and the winter types are ideal to cook with. As they grow so quickly, radishes are great to grow in unused spaces, or in the gaps between other vegetables before they get too large and shade the radishes. I use this intercrop method by growing rows of radishes between my cabbages; by doing this you get two crops from one bed. Radishes can also be used as marker plants for other, slower-growing plants such as parsnips. Simply sow your parsnips as usual, then sow a row of radishes at the side. The radish will germinate in a couple of days and show you where the rows are, meaning you won't accidentally plant in that bed or dig up the parsnip seed, which will take longer to germinate and become as visible as the radish seedlings.

Small red radishes are readily available in the shops, but there are long red ones with white tips, as well as purple, yellow, white, pink-centred and even black radishes to grow at home. In fact, did you know that in the original Peter Rabbit book, Peter was actually munching on a radish, not a carrot, in Mr McGregor's garden (you can tell from the leaves). This carrot-like root is an old variety named 'Long Scarlet'.

You can grow radishes almost anywhere, from open beds and borders to smaller containers and even window boxes and hanging baskets. Summer types can even be started early in a greenhouse or under cloches in late winter, sowing short rows every couple of weeks to keep a constant supply to harvest, whereas winter ones are sown in mid-summer and crop in autumn/winter.

How to grow

If growing in the open ground, make sure it's finely raked and free of any large stones, especially if you are growing a longer-shaped radish or mooli type. Create short drills 1cm (½in) deep. I usually make these around 1m (3ft) long as that's enough radishes for me in two weeks before I start another row, but make the row as long as you want, depending on how many you'll eat. Sow the seeds thinly around 1–2cm (½–¾in) apart, then as they germinate and grow you can thin your plants to around 2–3cm (¾–1¼in) apart, using the thinnings in salads, as the young leaves are also edible. If you are growing in containers just make sure they are sown 1cm (½in) deep and keep them moist, as they will grow quickly and consume all the water in the compost. It's best to avoid growing radishes in the height of summer as they can quickly bolt.

Winter radishes, also known as daikon, are sown the same way but should have 15cm (6in) between plants. They take around 10 weeks to mature and can be left in the ground longer than summer types.

◄ 'Felicia'

Harvesting and storing

Summer radishes should be harvested when they are young and juicy, normally within four weeks of sowing, otherwise they can become woody and tough. You can eat the young leaves of most radishes, although those with small hairs on the leaves are a little unpleasant, so only eat the smoother young ones. The roots can be kept in an airtight container on a piece of damp kitchen paper in the fridge, which will keep them fresh and crisp for longer. Winter radishes can be left in the soil until they are needed, or harvested in early winter and stored in boxes of damp sand throughout the winter.

Radishes to grow

Summer

'Felicia' – A long, purple-rooted radish with a white tip. This new purple-skinned variety is the perfect shape for snacking or slicing, crisp and with a milder flavour than most, it it good for those who find radishes too spicy.

'Long Scarlet' – A carrot-shaped, red radish with a punchy flavour. Taking slightly longer to crop than the smaller, round types, 'Long Scarlet' is good for snacking and salads and is delicious grated into slaw or homemade kimchi. Reaching up to 17cm (6½in) long, it's not just the root you can eat, but the peppery leaves too.

'18 Days' (De dix-huit jours) – A long, slender red radish with a white tip. Known as a 'French Breakfast' type, this root will crop 18–20 days from sowing, making it the ultimate speedy veg! Crisp and mild-flavoured, it can also be grown in the green-house earlier or later in the year. Best harvested when no longer than your thumb.

Winter

'Watermelon' – This is a Chinese heritage variety of daikon that has a white skin and green shoulders, hiding a bright pink centre that looks beautiful when sliced into rounds. Roots are crunchy and firm and can be harvested from golf-ball to tennis-ball-sized. Flavour-wise, it is milder and sweeter than hot and spicy, making it good for adding colour and crunch to autumn salads.

'China Rose' – This is a longer-shaped, rosy red root that has pure white flesh inside. Hardy to the cold, plants can be left in the ground until at least midwinter but will keep better if stored in boxes of damp sand. Punchier in flavour, this root is good for salads, while the leaves are a great addition to a stir-fry.

'Bluemoon' F1 – This has an eye-catching purple/blue skin, forming purple and white stripes internally when sliced into rounds. Best sown in late summer, these crunchy roots add a new colour to home-grown radish.

Problems

There are a couple of problems that can cause issues when growing radishes, but as they grow so quickly a few losses don't matter – you always have time to sow more.

Bolting can occur in the height of summer, especially if plants get stressed because they don't have enough water. Spring and autumn are the ideal times to grow radishes without fear of bolting, as they don't like the longer, hot days of summer; plus, when they bolt they become more bitter and woody. If you want to grow radishes during summer, sow your seeds in a shady place, such as behind bean plants, and keep them well watered.

Slugs and snails can decimate newly germinated seedlings, so consider using beer traps or copper tape to keep the pests away, or grow your plants in containers raised up off the ground or put your container on legs in large saucers of water to act as a moat.

Flea beetle can affect young radish plants, creating lots of small holes in the leaves. It may look unsightly, but it won't affect the eating quality of the roots, only the leaves. You can grow your plants under fine-mesh insect netting, or feed with a nitrogen-rich fertiliser to encourage the plants to produce more growth and outgrow the damage.

Top Tips

- If you have oilseed rape fields nearby, don't grow radishes in the garden during the middle of summer, or consider covering crops with insect-proof mesh. This is because the rapeseed will be harvested that month and any flae beetle on the crops will need a new host plant, zoning in on your radishes.

- If you are short on space, why not grow radishes in old guttering fixed to a wall or fence? Smaller, round varieties will work well in this situation.

◄ Radishes growing between slower growing brassicas

Parsnips

These root vegetables are closely related to carrots and parsley. They have a long, tapered shape and a creamy white to yellowish-tan skin. The flesh is firm and dense, with a sweet, nutty flavour that becomes more pronounced when cooked. They are a valuable root crop to grow at home, not just because they are tasty and versatile in the kitchen, but also because they are extremely hardy and can sit outside in the soil all winter and into spring. Notoriously difficult to get started, parsnip seeds should always be bought fresh each year to avoid disappointment. Plants can produce quite long roots and are best grown in the open ground, making sure the bed is stone-free and in a sunny position. Yet there are a couple of shorter varieties that can be grown in shallower soil, or even containers, making them accessible to gardeners who don't have a garden.

How to grow

Seeds can be sown from late winter onwards, yet it's more reliable to sow from early to late spring as parsnip seeds are fickle at germinating and the colder weather earlier in the year can cause failure. Make sure to add a bucket of well-rotted manure to every square metre of soil the autumn before sowing; while parsnips prefer fertile soil, freshly manured beds can cause roots to warp and twist. You can sow seeds in a shallow 1–2cm (½–¾in) deep drill, yet I find it easier to sow 3–4 seeds, 1cm (½in) deep at 15cm (6in) spacings in a row; you can then thin out your seedlings to a single plant as they grow.

The problem is, even sowing like this you can't ensure there will be a seedling produced at each spacing, which is why I start my seeds off in a plastic bag! This may seem strange, but by sowing in a ziplock bag, you can ensure all the seed you use will be viable and grow. To do this, place a damp piece of kitchen paper flat in the bag, then scatter your parsnip seeds on the paper, seal the bag and leave it in the house somewhere warm; it doesn't have to be dark, just out of direct sun. Keep checking the bag each day, and when you start to see a tiny white tail appear from your seeds, you know they are the ones that will grow as they are starting to produce a root. Germination can be slow and erratic, taking up to 30 days for signs of life to appear. At this point you need to carefully plant the seeds 15cm (6in) apart where you want them to grow, being careful not to snap or damage the little tail. Keep your plants moist and make sure they are weed-free, as parsnips don't like competition for nutrients.

Harvesting and storing

When the leaves of your plants begin to die back, they are ready to harvest; this is normally during autumn. As most of us use parsnips more in the winter, it's best to leave your plants in the ground and remove and compost the leaves as they die back. Once the roots have been frosted by the cold, they begin to develop a sweeter taste, so don't be worried that they will get harmed by the cold, as they are hardy. When lifting your roots, you will need a garden fork to dig longer roots without snapping them. You can then leave any you don't need in the loosened soil as they will be easier to harvest if the soil freezes later in the year. Alternatively, you can place the harvested roots in containers of compost or sand and store them in the shed or garage until you want to use them, as this prevents the struggle of trying to prise a parsnip from the frozen-solid garden!

▶ 'Sabre' F1

Parsnips to grow

'Sabre' F1 – This modern variety produces long, slender roots with a good colour and flavour. It may look like those you buy in the shops, but I've found it very reliable and easy to grow compared to some others. Roots can become quite large, yet they keep their flavour and texture without going woody.

'White Gem' – This British-bred variety has shorter roots than most, making it ideal for shallower soils and containers, as well as stonier sites. It has smooth white skin and is easy to peel, with a sweet, nutty taste. Resistant to canker.

'Kral Russian' – A rare heritage variety from Russia. The plants produce roots that have wider shoulders and slender roots, more like a beetroot or turnip shape than a parsnip. This unusual shape makes them excellent for growing in containers or shallow ground as they don't suffer damaged or stunted growth. This is also a great parsnip to grow in heavy, clay soil. Seeds are very rare.

'Hamburg Parsley' – Also known as turnip-rooted parsley or parsley root, this is a variety of parsley that is grown for its edible root. It is closely related to the curly and flat-leaf parsley commonly used in cooking, but it has a thicker, more robust root that is similar in appearance to a small parsnip or carrot and is cooked in the same way. This multi-use vegetable is little known, yet produces two crops from one plant and is well worth growing if you are short on space. Harvest the leaves in summer and wait until autumn before digging up the roots.

Problems

Canker is the main problem suffered by parsnips. It produces orange or dark patches on the root that are rough and usually start around the crown of the plant. Caused by a fungus, it is thought that drought and poorly draining soil can be the cause, and therefore adding sand to the site and ensuring consistent watering can help. If you suffer from canker on your site, it's best to grow canker-resistant varieties.

Carrot fly can also affect parsnips, with their dark, rough tunnels causing damage that can be confused for canker – yet you'll find carrot fly damage all down the root of the plant, not just on the shoulders. Growing plants under fine-mesh insect netting can help prevent the problem, or growing onions nearby can confuse and lessen attack as the fly can't smell the parsnips.

◄ Hamburg parsley
▼ Starting parsnip seeds on damp paper

Kohl Rabi

This is perhaps one of the strangest-looking vegetables you can grow at home; it has a round, bulb-like shape that grows above the ground, with a stem that rises up from the centre. The stem is topped with leaves that resemble those of collards or kale, giving it a UFO-shaped appearance. It can be peeled and sliced, diced or grated to add to salads, slaws or stir-fries. It can also be roasted, grilled or steamed as a side dish, or used in soups and stews. In fact, this incredibly versatile vegetable also has edible leaves that can be cooked like other leafy greens, meaning there is almost zero waste from this otherworldly plant. More drought-resistant than swedes and turnips, the root has a fresh, broccoli-like flavour, available in both green- and purple-skinned varieties. As they are quick-growing, you are best to sow a few more seeds every three weeks to keep a constant supply of roots throughout the summer and autumn. Unless growing a jumbo-sized variety that can get to the size of a football, the roots are at their best when golf-ball- to tennis-ball-sized, otherwise they lose flavour and become tough, with some becoming pithy or hollow in the middle.

How to grow

Seeds can be started directly outside in 1cm (½in) deep drills that are 30cm (12in) apart. Make sure the soil is weed-free and free-draining – you may need to add some sand if your garden has clay soil, or consider growing in raised beds or containers. As the seedlings begin to grow, they need to be thinned out until the plants are 15cm (6in) apart. Any seedlings that are removed can be transplanted elsewhere or used to plug gaps within the original drill. For an earlier crop you can sow seeds in modules in an unheated greenhouse from late winter, this is also a good way to grow plants if you suffer from a lot of slugs and snails, which can decimate newly germinated seedlings. Sow 2–3 seeds per cell, thinning to a single plant as they grow. Once the seedlings are around 5cm (2in) tall they should be hardened off and transplanted outside where they are to grow. Kohl rabi, like most other root vegetables, grow best when kept well watered throughout the growing season.

Harvesting and storing

When harvesting, simply cut from the little stem below the root. If you aren't using them straight away, they can be stored for a couple of weeks in the fridge. Remove the leaves, as they can be used as a green in their own right, or added to salads, then put the root into a plastic bag to preserve moisture. You can also freeze your kohl rabi; peel and blanch the root for 3 minutes in boiling water, then plunge into iced water to stop it cooking and to preserve the colour. Once cool, let them dry and freeze in airtight containers or plastic bags. A personal favourite way to preserve kohl rabi is to add it to the vegetable mix when making homemade piccalilli.

Kohl Rabi to Grow

'Kossak' F1 – This is a super-sized kohl rabi that can easily get to over 20cm (8in) wide, with some becoming as large as footballs and weighing 3kg (6½lb). A great choice for those who like to make slaws or salads, or for cutting into sticks for snacking and serving with dips. The roots stay tender and juicy even when large, never getting pithy or tough.

▶ 'Kolibri' F1

'Kolibri' F1 – Stunningly gorgeous, these deep violet coloured roots look amazing against their green foliage. Staying tender even when larger, this variety is also fast to crop, with edible roots being produced in less than 8 weeks.

Problems

Pests – like radish, kohl rabi suffer from slugs and snails, bolting and flea beetles, and you can take the same precautions to lessen damage (see page 42).

Caterpillars can also affect kohl rabi, but as the roots are so quick to grow, they are normally ready to harvest before the insect has done too much damage. However, it's a good idea to regularly inspect your plants for eggs and wipe them off the underside of the leaves if you find them.

see page 42

Top Tips

- Purple varieties are hardier than green, meaning they can be harvested right into autumn, while green varieties are at their best in summer.

- Kohl rabi can happily grow in semi-shade, allowing you to keep the sunniest spots for the neediest veg.

Jerusalem Artichokes (Perennial)

Also known as sunchokes, this root vegetable is native to North America. Despite its name, it is not actually an artichoke and has no relation to Jerusalem – in fact, it's related to the sunflower and can sometimes produce small, yellow, sunflower-like blooms if the summer is warm enough.

It's one of those vegetables you may see for sale now and again in farm shops – they look like fresh ginger (ginger root) and have a knobby, uneven shape. The skin is usually thin, and the flesh is white and crispy with a sweet and chestnut-like flavour and a slightly crunchy texture. The roots can be eaten raw or cooked, and they can be prepared in a variety of ways, such as roasted, grilled, boiled, mashed or pureed. They are also used to make stews, gratins and soups (delicious with a little fresh ginger in it); however, they contain a type of carbohydrate called inulin, which isn't easily broken down in our stomachs and can cause gas, hence the common name of 'fartichoke'! The plants can become quite tall, at least 2m (6½ft), but there are some new varieties that are as short as 60cm (2ft), and so are more suited for smaller beds or large pots. The advantage of growing Jerusalem artichokes on a large plot or allotment is that they can be used as a fast-growing screen to hide unsightly areas. That's why you'll normally find them at the side of the compost area – that, and the fact they like the nutrients that come from the decomposing waste. Plants can be grown as a perennial, coming back each year if you leave a few tubers in the ground, and they are extremely productive.

How to grow

This is perhaps one of the most resilient root vegetables, happily growing the following year from any missed tuber, so it's best to dig over the bed twice to remove all of them. When it comes to growing Jerusalem artichokes, remember they are prolific croppers, so you won't need masses of plants; in fact, 3–5 is usually ample. The tubers are available in spring, so you can either plant them straight out where they are to crop, in a weed-free bed that's had some added manure or compost, or start them in pots in an unheated greenhouse and plant them out in late spring. The tubers should be planted around 10–15cm (4–6in) deep and 30–40cm (12–16in) apart, depending on if you want to use them as a screen or not, with closer plantings creating a more solid feature. When the plants get to around 30–40cm (12–16in) tall it's a good idea to earth them up by dragging soil around the entire stem and pressing it down firmly to create a 15cm (6in) tall mound; this will help stabilise the plant in strong winds and prevent it blowing over.

Taller varieties will reach 2m (6½ft) tall in one season, so if you don't want them that tall, or you are on a windy site, you can cut them back to around 1.5m (5ft) tall with a pair of loppers. This will mean your plants are less prone to wind damage but will prevent them from producing their little sunflower blooms later in the year.

If growing in a pot, it's better to grow the shorter varieties, or prune your plants back to 1–1.5m (3–5ft) tall, which will slightly reduce your harvest, but not by much.

◄ Top left: spacing plants; Top right: digging a hole; Centre left: removing the seedling from the pot; Centre right: separating roots; Bottom left: planting; Bottom right: firming plants in

Harvest and storing

When it comes to harvesting and storing your artichokes, there's no better way to keep them than leaving them alone! As the leaves begin to yellow, chop the stems back to ground level, but don't compost them, instead lie them on top of the bed where the tubers are. By doing this you will not only remember where the plants are as you pass into winter, but the stems will also keep hard frost from freezing the soil too deeply, in turn protecting the tubers. Tubers will last a couple of weeks in the fridge in a sealed plastic bag, but for longer storage you can dig them up and put them in boxes of damp sand or compost in a frost-free shed or garage. This makes them easier to get to if the garden freezes solid, as it's no fun trying to harvest a few tubers when you can't get a spade in the frozen ground!

Jerusalem artichokes to grow

'Fuseau' – A tall variety reaching over 2m (6½ft) in height, perfect for larger plots and where a screen is needed. The tubers are slender, with a creamy skin, and very smooth, making them easy to peel. Large yields from a couple of plants.

'Dwarf' – Produces a tiny plant compared to all other artichokes, reaching 50–60cm (20–24in) tall, making it perfect for pots and raised beds. The tubers are a little knobbly with red skin, all produced around the central stem of the plant, so they are easier to harvest and less invasive as they don't spread far.

'Dwarf Sunray' – A shorter 1.5–1.8m (5–6ft) tall variety, but what makes it special is the fact that it's the most reliable to flower in the UK, producing small, palm-sized yellow 'sunflowers' for several months in the summer. The tubers are white, with a nutty flavour.

Problems

Slugs can be an issue when plants are grown in the open ground, creating holes in the tubers while they are still growing. If your garden is prone to slugs you may want to consider using nematodes – little parasites – against them, as that's the only way you can get rid of them under the ground.

Wind rock (see page 60) can also be a problem for taller plants. You can earth up the stems, provide supports with stakes or grow your plants by a fence, wall or other structure so you can tie them in for support if bad weather is forecast.

◀ 'Fuseau'

Oca

Also known as New Zealand yam, this is a root vegetable native to the Andes mountains in South America but also cultivated in New Zealand. The tubers come in a variety of bright colours, including red, orange, yellow, pink, white and bicoloured, leading to the common name 'Jewels of the Andes'. Small, at roughly the size of a baby potato, and having a knobbly, irregular shape, oca produce short little plants that look like shamrocks or clover, and are suitable to grow in containers or in the open ground. The leaves are also edible, having a lemony tang (like sorrel) that works well when added to salads, although don't harvest too many as this may affect the yield of tubers below ground. The tubers themselves can be eaten raw, having a lemony flavour and nice crunch like a carrot, which is great for salads. However, the zesty flavour disappears when cooked, becoming nuttier and taking on the texture of beetroot rather than potatoes – I like them roasted in a little oil with salt and pepper. Even the stems of the plant can be eaten as you would rhubarb in pies or crumbles, having that typically rhubarb-sour taste. Stunningly beautiful, oca really does seem to be one of those 'lost foods' that more people should grow, as they are hardly ever seen for sale, easy to care for and suffer from hardly any problems at all; and unlike their potato and tomato cousins they won't succumb to blight either!

How to grow

Oca is grown very much like potatoes, just with a few differences – the main one being the need for free-draining soil to thrive, so raised beds and large pots (40cm/16in wide) work well. You can wait for the soil to warm up before planting tubers in the ground in late spring around 8cm (3in) deep with at least 60cm (2ft) between them. Keep them covered with fleece until they are established in early summer, then they can be uncovered. I personally think it's better to start them off earlier in late winter/early spring. At that time, tubers can be started individually in 15cm (6in) pots in a greenhouse or on a windowsill, then keep the plants frost-free and plant them out when all chance of frost has passed and the soil has begun to warm up. As the plants grow, they will flop to the ground a little, where the stems can root and start to produce more tubers, which can be earthed up like potatoes to increase yield later in the year. Don't worry if tubers are exposed to sunlight, as they don't go green like potatoes; in fact, they can become sweeter.

Keep your plants well watered, especially when the weather is dry; this can be done with a mulch of grass clippings around the plant in summer, helping prevent water evaporation. You may even be rewarded with small yellow flowers later in the season. These too are edible, with a milder flavour than the tubers.

▶ 'Dylan Keating' and 'Giggles'

Harvesting and storing

Oca tubers don't begin to swell and get bigger until daylight hours reduce, meaning you must wait until the leaves have died back, then wait at least two weeks for the tubers to reach their optimum size before harvesting. Covering the plants with fleece or a cloche will extend the time during which tubers are produced. Covering the bed with fleece will prevent any tubers near the surface suffering frost damage. The tubers will be produced near the surface and should all come up together when loosened with a fork. Once harvested, the tubers should be washed, dried and left on a sunny windowsill for a week. This process reduces the natural oxalic acid content that produces the lemony taste and makes the tubers sweeter; they can then be stored like potatoes in a cool, dark place until needed. Alternatively, if you are on well-draining soil, you can leave the tubers in the ground with a covering of leaves and fleece to protect them from frost, and they will then last until beyond Christmas (in the UK).

Oca to grow

'Dylan Keating' – Produces very attractive, creamy, yellow skin with red markings around the eyes. Tubers are more egg-shaped and larger than most, with a smooth skin. This not only means you get a larger harvest, but the tubers are also easier to clean.

'Giggles' – These have a rich, red skin with cream and yellow around the eyes. It has a more elongated shape and produces lots of smaller-sized tubers with a smooth skin.

There are many types of oca for sale by colour rather than name, and you can even buy edible tubers and grow from them.

Problems

The only real problem that oca suffer from is slug damage on the tubers, just like potatoes do. This is usually because of the keel slug and can be controlled with nematodes. Growing your plants in a raised bed will also reduce the chances of damage.

Top Tips

- If you aren't ready to plant your tubers when they arrive, they can be chitted like potatoes.

- If your tubers produce long shoots before planting, placing them on a light windowsill should prevent them growing any more. However, if you remove a couple of shoots they can be placed in a glass of water to root, giving you more plants for free.

- To keep the bejewelled colours of your oca, serve it raw, as cooking will quickly drain the colour from the skin, leaving it a creamy colour.

◄ Oca foliage

Brassicas

Sometimes seen as less important than other types of veg, cabbages and other members of their family are fantastic vegetables to grow in the garden or on an allotment – in fact, you can even squeeze a few of the smaller-sized varieties into a smaller veg patch. Unfortunately, they are out of bounds for a windowsill gardener, unless you want to grow them as microgreens.

There really isn't that much point in growing bog-standard white cabbages, which are cheap to buy, unless you have lots of space or really love cabbage; instead, why not grow one that is thin-leaved and ultra-crispy – perfect to use in place of lettuce in salads, and fast becoming a favourite in trendy restaurants. From cabbage to cauliflower, kale to broccoli, there are varieties out there that are a feast for your eyes and your tummy: from orange, purple and pink cauliflowers to white-sprouting broccoli, red Brussels sprouts and even perennial kales that grow to become giants!

Cabbages

When you think of this unassuming plant, don't remember the over-boiled veg you were served at school, instead imagine the delicious and nutritious coleslaw, salads, wraps, krauts, soups and traditional bubble and squeak that you can make with it. Available in several different shapes, colours and sizes, cabbages are a versatile vegetable and quite easy to grow; you can almost harvest a cabbage any day of the year if you grow a selection of varieties. When it comes to choosing your cabbage, there are a few main types to pick from, including pointed, round, Savoy and red. All are sown and grown in the same way, it's just a case of different sowing times and planting distances to accommodate the different-sized plants.

How to grow

Personally, I like to start my cabbage seed off in small modules or cell trays to give them the best chance of success and to prevent slugs and other critters devouring my seedlings, which tends to happen if they are started in a seedbed or directly in the soil. By starting your seeds like this you can make sure you get the most from a packet of seeds, as some of the modern F1 varieties can be pricey (but they are worth the money). Using a good-quality peat-free compost, I sow my seeds 1–2cm (½–¾in) deep with 2 seeds per cell, keep the compost moist and leave them in the unheated greenhouse or cold frame, or on a kitchen windowsill, to germinate. Once they have started to grow you should thin seedlings to single plant per cell, but don't waste the smaller seedlings; you can transplant them to their own cell for extra plants, if you like.

Cabbages grow best in a sunny bed of alkaline to neutral soil, so test your soil's pH if you don't know it (you can buy kits for this at garden centres or online), and if it's too acidic, add some garden lime to the beds – just follow the guidance on the packet for how much to apply. You'll also produce better cabbages if you enrich your growing space with compost or manure before planting; a bucket or two per square metre will do the trick, just don't add manure and lime at the same time as they can release ammonia gas and nitrogen from the soil. Ideally, you should manure in the autumn before planting in spring, to allow the bed to settle. Next, you need to do the 'cabbage shuffle'; this involves standing on the bed and treading the soil down to compact it , then shuffling back and forth to make sure the entire bed is nice and firm. Cabbages prefer this and it prevents them suffering 'wind rock', which is when the plant moves around in the wind, snapping the small roots that take up nutrients so that it can't grow properly and produces just a small plant.

▶ 'Marquess' F1

▶ Top left: removing seed leaves; Top right: transplanting seedling deeply; Centre left: fitting cabbage collar; Centre right: firiming in; Bottom left: harvesting with a serrated knife; Bottom right: bonus crop of leaves in the stump after cutting

When the seedlings are large enough to handle, normally 10–15cm (4–6in) tall, and have a couple of true leaves, it's time to plant them out. Prepare the planting hole a little deeper than you usually would so that you can transplant the seedling deep into the ground. Cabbages can be planted up to just below their first true leaves, which makes them more stable in the soil. If you need to remove seed leaves that haven't naturally dropped, just snip them off before planting. Space your plants 30–45cm (12–18in) apart depending on the variety and what the seed packet recommends; normally, the smaller the cabbage the closer they can be planted. Once the seedlings are in place, 'puddle' them in by pouring water gently into the hole – this will result in soil packing tightly around the seedlings without the fear of any damage to them. Firm the plants in and water again, keeping them moist as they grow, especially in dry periods.

Harvest and storing

When it comes to harvesting, there is no set rule, they just need to be the size you want. If you want fresh greens but your plant hasn't formed a dense heart yet, that's fine, just harvest it and use it like spring greens. I use an old bread knife to cut the head from the stem, as it's much easier with a serrated knife than a flat blade or secateurs. Afterwards, if you don't need the bed for other crops straight away, cut a 1cm (½in) deep cross in the top of the stem where you removed the cabbage, and in a few weeks the plant will have produced small fresh leaves that can be harvested for a bonus crop!

Cabbages to grow

Round cabbages
Forget the standard white cabbages you can buy so cheaply in the supermarkets, and instead opt for one of the new types, which are thin-leaved, sweet and extra crisp.

'Cabbice' F1 – A fantastic cabbage to use as a lettuce substitute. It produces tightly packed, dense heads with thin and crispy leaves, which are sweet-tasting, making them ideal for use in salads or coleslaw. It has a flatter shape rather than round, meaning the leaves come away easily and form a natural bowl shape, which is good to fill and roll to make a delicious wrap.

'Green Rich' F1 – Very similar to 'Cabbice', yet it hearts up at a much smaller size, meaning you can harvest small heads that are the size of your palm; perfect for a smaller site or if there are only two of you to feed. That said, they will continue to grow, reaching 1.5–2kg (3¼–4½lb) when mature.

Top Tip

- As a rough guide:
  – summer cabbages are sown between late winter and late spring and transplanted late spring/ early summer – winter cabbages are sown mid–late spring and transplanted early–mid-summer – spring cabbages are sown mid–late summer, transplanted early–mid-autumn, and left to grow all winter before harvesting the next spring.

- Add a cabbage collar around the base of all your brassica seedlings; this prevents cabbage root fly from laying their eggs where the plant meets the soil, which in turn prevents the larvae from eating the seedlings' roots and killing them. A piece of old carpet or any thick material will work if it's a snug fit; just cut a circle or square 10–15cm (4–6in) in diameter from the fabric, make a slit from one side to the middle and fit the collar around the stem of each plant. for more tips, see page 85.

Savoy cabbages

The hardiest of all cabbages, these can happily sit outside through frost and snow, making them invaluable in the veg patch, as they'll keep cropping until late spring.

'Rigoletto' F1 – A hardy cabbage that can stand all winter, surviving down to -20°C (-4°F)! Ideal to grow through the colder months; the outer leaves can be removed to reveal a deliciously tender cabbage that's perfect for any winter meal, but particularly good in bubble and squeak because of the puckered leaves.

'D'Aubervilliers' – This is a rare, old French variety which is mild-tasting and very tender. Originating near Paris in the town of Aubervilliers, this cabbage has beautiful, crinkly leaves and is amazing when simply cooked in butter and sprinkled with sea salt.

Pointed cabbages

These are commonly known as 'sweetheart' cabbages, due to their much sweeter flavour compared to other types.

'Winterjewel' F1 – This bucks the trend and crops in spring, happily growing outside during winter. This sweet-tasting variety can be harvested early as spring greens or left to heart up into a loose-headed cabbage. It's a versatile and valuable plant to grow as it can be eaten at different stages over a long time.

'Marquess' F1 – A modern variety that holds its shape for longer in the ground, whereas some pointed types can split if they get too big. It can be harvested at almost any size, with 500g (18oz) being the ideal weight. This autumn-cropping cabbage has fewer outer leaves, making it good to grow in smaller spaces or closer together to produce smaller heads.

'Kalibos' – Just about the only pointed red cabbage available. It's got very few outer leaves, meaning it grows in smaller spaces. This cabbage has the sweetness of a pointed cabbage and the intense colour of a red, making it good to use raw in salads, or to make a sweeter pickled cabbage.

Red cabbages

Not always as popular as its paler cousins, red cabbage is great for pickling or braising with apples for hearty winter dinners, or the Christmas table.

'Pink Star' F1 – This is an innovation for red cabbages, as it has the same crunch and taste, yet it has been bred to create a plant that doesn't bleed when cut, like other red cabbages. This not only means you won't get red hands, but your coleslaw and salads will also stay fresh, without going pink! Extra crispy, great for adding colour to salads or homemade sauerkraut.

'Pretino' F1 – Ideal for smaller spaces, this cabbage has a smaller core than other reds, meaning more edible leaves and less waste. The plants heart up early, so it can be harvested when just a bit bigger than a tennis ball – the perfect size for serving two.

Club-root-resistant varieties

'Kilazol' F1 (round) – A good round cabbage for autumn harvesting.

'Cordesa' F1 (Savoy) – The first club-root-resistant Savoy, with heavily crinkled leaves and a compact habit.

'Lodero' F1 (red) – A small to medium-sized cabbage with intense red/purple leaves; perfect to eat raw, cooked or when pickled.

▶ Top left and right: 'Pretino' F1; bottom left and right: 'Green Rich' F1

Cauliflowers

Cauliflower has a reputation for being a challenging vegetable to cultivate in the garden, yet with a few simple precautions you can increase your chances of producing perfect plants. Despite its reputation, its versatility in the kitchen should not be overlooked. While it is often associated with the classic dish cauliflower cheese, this multifunctional vegetable can be used in a variety of ways. For instance, it is a key ingredient in homemade piccalilli, adding small chunks of texture to the turmeric- and mustard-spiced sauce, and it is also a staple in the popular aloo gobi curry, which combines soft potatoes with flavourful cauliflower pieces. Although traditionally boiled, cauliflower is now appreciated in its raw form with dips or transformed into 'rice' as a low-carb alternative.

With a growing number of gardeners discovering its potential, this allotment favourite is attracting new fans throughout the UK, especially as it is available in shades of green, bright purple, violet and even orange! The vibrant colours of these kaleidoscopic cauliflowers look incredible served with dips on a platter or tossed through a late-summer salad.

How to grow

If you want to grow cauliflowers successfully, there are a few essential things to keep in mind that can help prevent disaster. First, it's crucial to choose the right cauliflower variety for the season, as not all varieties can be grown simultaneously, and some perform better than others at certain times of the year. Check the seed packet to see when you can sow and harvest the plants and try to stick to these guidelines as closely as possible. Some varieties are better sown in spring, while others should be sown in autumn, grown through winter, and then harvested the following spring. Certain varieties, such as 'All The Year Round,' can be grown for almost 12 months of the year by being sown successively in spring and autumn.

You can start off the seed in a seedbed, but it's better to do this in trays or modules, particularly for more expensive F1 varieties, to protect the seedlings from hungry slugs. Cauliflowers are quite hardy and don't require additional heat to get started – an unheated greenhouse or cold frame with a temperature of around 8–10°C (46–50°F) is sufficient to produce stocky plants that can withstand harsh weather conditions.

Sow the seeds about 0.5cm (¼in) deep in high-quality compost, and they should germinate in around 14 days. Once the seedlings are large enough to handle, either pot them on or transplant them from the seedbed to where they will grow, spacing them 50–75cm (20–30in) apart, depending on the type of cauliflower. As a rule, summer/autumn cropping varieties should be planted around 60cm (24in) apart, while overwintering varieties should be planted up to 75cm (30in) apart to allow for greater airflow during the wetter months, which can help prevent leaf rot and the spread of disease. If you want to grow single-serving-sized cauliflowers, plant summer varieties 30cm (12in) apart. This will force them to produce smaller, tennis-ball-sized curds.

▶ 'Andromeda' F1

Regardless of the planting distance, ensure that the soil is as fertile as possible, as this is one of the keys to success with cauliflowers. Add a bucket of well-rotted manure per square metre to the cauliflower beds, fork it through thoroughly, then tread the soil flat and compact. This may seem strange, as most plants don't thrive in compacted soil, but these plants prefer a firm, solid ground as excessive movement in the wind can cause the curd to 'blow' and open, rather than remain tight.

Cauliflowers can be planted in the same way as cabbages, firmed in well and fitted with a cabbage collar (see page 63). Cauliflowers can be thirsty, and any growth interruption due to the plants becoming dry will cause the curds to be smaller, so water well after planting and keep them well watered through-out their lives, particularly in dry weather. Once the plants have established, and before the curd starts to form, it's essential to add a high-nitrogen fertiliser such as sulphate of ammonia to assist with curd formation. A dosage of 20–30g (¾–1¾oz) per square metre is usually adequate – simply rake it through the topsoil surrounding the plants.

Problems

If you've ever grown cauliflowers that have turned grey or yellow, there are two potential reasons for this: slugs and sun. Slugs can graze on the surface of the curd, causing it to discolour and become scarred. To prevent this, take appropriate measures to control the pesky critters and keep them away from your cauliflowers (see page 85). On the other hand, sunlight can also discolour older cauliflower varieties, so it's important to cover the forming curd with its own leaves. You can do this by either using clothes pegs to hold the leaves together over the curd or by snapping the midrib of the leaves and bending them over on themselves to prevent light penetrating through. If this seems like too much work, consider growing one of the coloured-curd varieties – the curds become even more vibrant when exposed to sunlight and taste just as good as white ones. However, if you boil the purple ones, they may turn blue during cooking, so to preserve their colours try steaming, stir-frying or roasting them instead.

Top Tips

· You can use clothes pegs to hold the leaves over traditional white-headed varieties, which prevents the sun getting to the curd and turning it yellow-grey.

· The young leaves and crunchy central core of cauliflowers are delicious, so don't compost them; they make great additions to a stir-fry or salad.

◄ Top left: harvesting cauliflower; Top right: removing excess leaves; Bottom left: checking for any hidden slugs; Bottom right: cauliflower ready for the kitchen!

Cauliflowers to grow

'Depurple' F1 – A striking, violet-lavender cauliflower that really does stand out in the garden, becoming brighter coloured when the sunlight is allowed to get to the curd. With a nutty, buttery taste, this variety will keep its colour if lightly steamed or stir-fried, or why not enjoy it raw in salads and with dips?

'Graffiti' F1 – A deep purple cauliflower that can grow pretty large when grown in nutrient-rich soil. It needs full sun exposure to the head for the maximum depth of colour, which means there is no need to cover the curd. Cropping later than 'Depurple', this variety has a deeper, darker colour than its earlier-harvesting, lavender-coloured counterpart.

'Sunset' F1 – A vibrant orange-coloured cauliflower with tight curds and a semi-upright habit. The colour is more intense when the plant is smaller, so they are ideal for using as baby veg; however, the colour does remain as the plant matures, making them great for cauliflower cheese as they add an extra burst of orange!

'Green Storm' F1 – Produces lime-green-headed cauliflowers that really do make you stand back and think, 'What? Wait a minute, it's GREEN!' Again, this is another cauliflower that must be appreciated for its beauty and should ideally be eaten raw to show it off. Blitzed up into cauliflower rice, it can be mixed through couscous salads to add a burst of colour as well as a nutty flavour.

'Andromeda' F1 – This may be a regular white-headed cauliflower, yet it's one of the easiest to grow as the head stays brilliant white even if it's not covered from the sun, never going yellow when it reaches maturity. It is not only easy to grow, but also less prone to slug damage, as the menacing molluscs aren't able to hide under the folded leaves. Personally, I think this is one of the best white-headed cauliflowers available, as it needs less attention.

'Clapton' F1 – A pure-white, club-root-resistant variety that is well protected by its leaves. Maturing over several weeks, it won't give you a glut of cauliflower all at once in the autumn.

◄ Top: 'Green Storm' F1; Centre: 'Depurple' F1; Bottom: 'Sunset' F1

Cauliflower's crazy-looking cousin

Along with the regular-shaped cauliflower, there's also the amazingly shaped Romanesco cauliflower, which is sometimes called a broccoli. This beautiful vegetable has conical-shaped florets that spiral out from a central point to form a fractal-like pattern, looking almost like a work of art. They are grown in the same way as other cauliflowers and come in shades of green, white or orange; perfect to serve as unusual crudités or roasted as a delicious side dish.

Romanesco cauliflowers to grow

'Veronica' F1 – This is perhaps the go-to Romanesco for growing in the UK, producing pale, lime-green heads that look stunning in salads or simply steamed on a plate. Growing taller than regular cauliflowers, reaching up to 90cm (3ft) tall, plants have an upward-facing leaf habit that wraps the head well. This variety is nuttier in flavour and crunchier in texture than cauliflowers.

'Amo 125' F1 – A modern, sunshine-orange Romanesco from Italy that isn't just vibrant on the outside; the colour remains on the inside as well – even when cooked. This autumn-harvesting variety is a total eye-catcher, with everyone who sees it wanting to know 'what is it, where can I get it?' I've used this variety to add colour and interest to homemade piccalilli, because the unusual conical shape really stands out.

▲ 'Veronica' F1

Kales

Once relegated to cattle and animal feed, kale is now seen as a superfood by many celebrities and influencers, yet we gardeners have enjoyed it for years! This delicious and nutritious leafy plant is well at home on an allotment or in the veg patch, and you can even grow baby leaves on a windowsill.

Usually found for sale in the supermarket labelled as 'curly kale', with tightly curled green leaves, kale comes in green, purple, near-black and even bicoloured. One of my favourite types is the traditional Tuscan black (cavolo nero, which translates as 'black cabbage'), with slender, Savoy-puckered leaves in a dark green, almost black colour. Traditionally used in minestrone soup, this tasty kale keeps its shape and texture when cooked, as opposed to other members of the cabbage family, which go mushy when cooked for too long.

When it comes to curly kale, you could grow the green varieties, like those sold in the shops, but why not take the opportunity to grow the more attractive red/purple types or those with green leaves and red midribs, such as 'Midnight Sun'? As most kales are winter hardy, it pays to grow a more attractive-looking variety in the veg patch, as it adds some well-needed colour to the plot in the bleaker months. For those who love kale and could eat it all year round, try a perennial variety that will produce leaves 365 days a year, growing to become rather large garden plants.

How to grow

Seeds can be sown from early spring to early summer in modules or seed trays in an unheated greenhouse or cold frame; they don't need any extra heat as this can result in the seedlings becoming leggy and tall. Sow seeds thinly, 1cm (½in) deep in a seed tray, or 2 per cell if you're using a module tray. After a couple of weeks your seedlings should have germinated, and once they get to around 7cm (2¾in) tall it's time to thin the seedlings to 1 per cell, or remove weak seedlings from the tray – the thinnings are delicious added to a salad or sandwich. Once your seedlings have several true leaves and are 10–15cm (4–6in) tall, they can be transplanted to their final growing positions around 45cm (18in) apart, planting deeper – as you do with cabbages – and fitting a cabbage collar around the base of the plant (see pages 63 and 85). It also pays to cover the plants with fine-mesh insect netting, as whitefly can attack kale plants, and because of the curly nature of the leaf it's difficult to wash them off, so prevention is better than cure.

Harvesting and storing

When harvesting, it's best to cut the leaves with secateurs or a sharp knife, taking a couple of leaves from each plant as opposed to cutting them off at the ground like you would a cabbage. Cropping them this way gives your plants time to produce more leaves and extends the harvest time. If you want to store kale without it going limp, wash it under running water and shake most of it off, then seal the leaves in a ziplock bag or other container and it will happily keep in the fridge for 7–10 days.

▶ 'Midnight Sun'

Kales to grow

'Yurok' F1 – This is a cavolo nero type of kale, yet it's more compact that the original, making it much more suited for growing in a smaller garden. The slender, puckered leaves are also known as 'dinosaur kale', because the leaf pattern is said to resemble dinosaur skin. It's more mildew-resistant than most kales, plus the leaves don't yellow, meaning less waste. This kale is the one for gardeners who are short on space but want big crops.

'Frost Byte' F1 – This resembles a more relaxed curly kale as it grows, with light green leaves that are waved around the edges. As the plant matures and grows through the colder months, the leaves change to a beautiful ice white at the growing tip, giving rise to the plant's name. The white leaves are not only thinner and more tender, but they are also sweeter.

'Redbor' F1 – An extremely curly, rich-purple-leaved kale that is very winter hardy, giving plenty of interest to the veg patch throughout winter, and also adds colour to your plate. The leaves are not only delicious cooked, but the younger leaves can be harvested and added raw to autumn salads. A little taller than some other kales, this 90cm (3ft) plant even looks great planted in the flower border, where it adds interest in the colder months. Rarely seen for sale in the supermarket, red curly kale is becoming more popular with allotmenteers around the UK.

'Midnight Sun' – This has a dark pink midrib running through green ruffled leaves, and a sweeter taste than most. This attractive kale can also be used smaller in salads and works well as a baby leaf grown on a windowsill; let them grow into larger plants outside and they will crop all winter, into spring.

'Rainbow Candy Crush' F1 – An extremely attractive kale, with an almost ornamental stature. It is shorter than most, with very little space between the internodes (the space between two nodes, or joints), so it looks a little like an ornamental cabbage. Dark green leaves surround the pinky-purple centre, and both colours show on each leaf. It's not as hardy as other kales, as this one doesn't like frost that much, but it adds an ornamental kitchen-garden look to anywhere it's grown.

◄ Top: perennial kale in flower border;
Bottom: kale plants inside insect netting

Perennial kale

'Daubenton's' (perennial) – This perennial kale comes in both solid green and variegated green-and-cream-leaved (known as 'Panache'), and can survive for many years in the garden. Perennial kales don't produce viable seeds, so they are best grown from plants or stem cuttings, which is why you hardly ever see them for sale as a plant or as a vegetable in the shops. Common in kitchen gardens until Victorian times, perennial kales are making a comeback with allotmenteers and gardeners alike, who are trying to get their hands on cuttings to root at home. Growing wide (at up to 2m/6½ft), the plants are quite a task to net, so it's a relief to know they don't seem to be as bothered by pests as regular kales and even when they are attacked, they shrug it off easily. If you make space for this plant, you can grow it out of the way, and you'll be eating kale whenever you like. You can even take cuttings easily from mid-autumn to early summer – simply cut a side shoot that has knobbly ridges, remove the larger leaves and push it into a pot of compost two-thirds deep. Within a few weeks it will start to root, and as soon as the roots stick out of the base of the pot, it's ready to transplant into the garden or gift to a friend. They really are easy to propagate, with little effort.

Top Tips

- Mulch around plants to keep them moist during the summer, then you'll have to water them less. It also helps to keep the plants weed-free.

- Certain types of kale, especially cavolo nero varieties, will start to produce sprouting broccoli-like spears if they are left in the ground over winter until late spring. This bonus crop is well worth waiting for, as it can't be bought in the shops and has the unique taste of kale, but with the texture and look of broccoli!

Brussels Sprouts

If there is one vegetable that can divide opinion between the best of friends, or even lead to family arguments, it must be the Brussels sprout. Traditionally they were bitter-tasting, leading them to be boiled for what seemed like hours before they were served, resembling a soft, green ball. Nowadays, modern breeding means the bitterness has gone and you're left with a delicious, firm yet silky sphere of goodness. I must admit, I'm a lover of sprouts and can't get enough of them, especially when simply roasted in the oven with a drizzle of olive oil and balsamic; they go charred and crisp on the outside and stay velvety on the inside, delicious! Needing around 50cm (20in) square each, you can fit a plant or two into just about the smallest of gardens, even planting them in the centre of a raised bed and growing lower crops like lettuce around them, as they won't mind the shade given by the taller Brussels. Traditionally all Brussels sprouts produced green buttons (that's what the little sprouts are really called), yet we can now grow red, almost purple, varieties as well, which have a nuttier flavour to them and look very attractive when served.

Sautéing or lightly steaming red sprouts will help them to keep the most colour when cooked, or they can be shredded and added to coleslaw in the autumn months. You'll also find that the flavour of all Brussels sprouts becomes sweeter after your plants have been frosted a couple of times as the weather gets colder. However, as modern breeding allows you to start cropping from late summer, this isn't as noticeable as it is with older varieties.

How to grow

It's best to add well-rotted manure or homemade compost to the bed in which you want to grow your plants, which should be done in the autumn or early spring before planting. Seeds were traditionally sown straight into the garden, but with the price of more modern F1 seed this can be expensive if your seedlings get eaten. Therefore, I always start mine in module trays with 2 seeds per cell, sown 1cm (½in) deep in good-quality peat-free compost. You can leave the tray in an unheated greenhouse, cold frame or in the shed by the window to germinate; but whatever you do, don't keep your newly sown seeds too warm, or they will become leggy and weak. Brussels can germinate and grow in lower temperatures, producing stocky plants with good root systems, whereas if you leave them on a warm windowsill you end up with tall, soft plants with fewer roots.

When your plants are 10–15cm (4–6in) tall, usually in early–mid-summer, you can plant them out where they will grow, transplanting seedlings 50–60cm (20–24in) apart and firming the soil around them well before watering in. If you are growing a taller variety or your site is exposed to the wind, it's worth pushing in a sturdy stick or pole next to each plant, as this will allow you to support it as it grows. Keeping your plants secure is key when growing sprouts, as any movement (wind rock) can cause the buttons to 'blow', which means they don't stay nice and solid and instead puff up and almost look like a tiny cabbage. In summer, as the plants are growing, it's good to add some extra feed in the form of chicken manure pellets (around 150g/5oz per square metre). This nitrogen-rich boost will help get the best from your plants, then as late summer arrives you can mound up soil around the base of your plants to add a little more stability.

During the growing season I always remove any yellowing or damaged leaves, as this takes away hiding places for slugs and snails, while also preventing the build-up of any pathogens in the surrounding soil.

Harvesting and storing

When it comes to harvesting, pick buttons from the bottom of the plant, as they will be the biggest, and this gives the others time to swell.

Don't forget the tops! The tops of your plants will have formed a small, cabbage-like crown; these are delicious and never seen for sale in the shops. When you start to harvest the buttons, cut the top from the plant and eat it as you would cabbage or spring greens – it tastes mildly of sprouts. Removing it from the plant encourages the smaller, higher-up buttons to swell and get bigger.

Brussels sprouts to grow

'Red Rubine' – This deep purple Brussels sprout is a real eye-catcher on the plate and in the garden. It's totally different to what we all think of as a sprout, with a nuttier taste that works well when roasted with chestnuts around Christmas time.

'Marte' F1 – This green variety produces some of the largest buttons I've ever seen, almost as big as a hen's egg! Great roasted, but also a good sprout to shred for coleslaw. Can be harvested from mid-autumn to mid-winter. Imagine the look on your family's face when they get one or two of these whoppers on their plate!

'Kalettes' – This is a cross between two superfoods: kale and Brussels sprouts! These crazy-shaped veg have a wavy edge like kale and produce what look like tiny cabbages instead of traditional tight buttons. Having green leaves that graduate to purple, you can see why these British-bred beauties are so popular. Not only that, they also provide twice the vitamins B, C and E than a standard Brussels sprout!

'Crispus' F1 – This disease-resistant variety will easily shrug off club root if you suffer from it on your plot, happily producing lots of delicious, dark green buttons in autumn.

Top Tip

- Add a sturdy stake to the side of the plant and tie it in with garden twine to stop any wind rock. You can also mound soil up around the base of the plant and tread it firm to help do the same job.

◄ Removing the top of the plants

When most of us think of broccoli, we think of the green domed vegetable that sadly often comes wrapped in plastic in the supermarket. Yet there are also purple-flushed varieties, stem broccoli, sprouting broccoli and more. What we class as regular broccoli are plants that produce that one big head to harvest and use up within a few days, which are great for larger families or those who eat lots of broccoli.

Stem broccoli starts off life looking the same as regular broccoli, producing a large head that can be harvested at that stage or left on the plant to produce individual stems. Once the head forms, it begins to split, elongate and carry on growing, producing lots of slender stems that are marketed as Tenderstem® in the supermarket. The great thing about these plants is that you can snap as many stems from the plant as you like, while leaving the remainder for another day; plus you can grow green or burgundy varieties to give you variation in colour. As regular broccoli is readily available all year round, I would urge you to grow stem broccoli as an alternative, which allows you to harvest a whole head, if you like, or leave the plant to produce the sweeter stems. By making the change it will also extend your harvest period, giving you two different harvests over several weeks.

Sprouting broccoli are usually larger plants that need longer in the ground, sometimes almost a year, making them only suitable for larger gardens and allotments where the bed won't be needed again in a hurry. These are what we usually see for sale as purple sprouting broccoli, though they do come in white as well, with late winter being the prime time for harvest. While they may take up space, plants will produce a constant supply of slender shoots for quite a few weeks, meaning you get more per plant than from a regular broccoli.

There is even a perennial broccoli that looks like a cauliflower! This plant will produce around nine creamy-white, tennis-ball-sized heads a year and keep cropping for five years or more.

How to grow

When it comes to sowing and growing broccoli, it's very similar to all the other cabbage family members, with the most important thing being when to sow. You can get varieties that crop in summer, autumn, winter and spring, so checking on the seed packet for sowing dates is critical, otherwise you may find your plants bolt prematurely and you don't get as good a harvest as you should. Taking what space you have into consideration is also a major factor when growing broccoli – sprouting types are sometimes in the ground for 12 months from one spring to the next, so that bed will be taken up for the entire year.

All broccoli performs better in soil that is fertile and well-drained, so adding well-rotted manure to the bed the autumn before planting will increase your harvest dramatically. Plants also prefer a sunny site, so make sure you give them prime position, if possible.

Broccoli

Due to slugs and birds easily decimating germinating seeds, I always start my seeds off in trays or modules in a cold frame, as this allows me to transplant strong little seedlings where I want them to grow. Sow the seeds 1cm (½in) deep, and once plants are 10–15cm (4–6in) tall they can be planted out. Take care of planting distances, as some varieties need around 70–90cm (2½–3ft) between them. For this reason, plants are best grown in raised beds or the open ground, as they don't perform well in pots. Broccolis are transplanted and cared for like cauliflowers, with cabbage collars and netting being a must if you want to keep your plants pest-free (see pages 63 and 85).

Broccoli to grow

Stem broccoli

'Hirzia' F1 – This compact plant only grows to 40–50cm (16–20in) tall, producing a traditional green broccoli head that can be harvested at that stage or left to split into stems. Within a week you will be able to harvest sweet-tasting spears of tenderstem broccoli, taking as many as you need while leaving the rest on the plant for another day. The spears are great eaten raw in salads or stir-fries.

'Purple Rain' F1 – A purple-headed broccoli with green stems that can be harvested as one large head or left to split into smaller spears that look just like purple sprouting broccoli. This British-bred variety will crop from summer to autumn if you make a couple of sowings, making it both attractive and productive in the garden. The spears will lose their purple colour if cooked for too long, so lightly steaming, stir-frying or eating them raw is the best way to preserve the pigment.

'Purplelicious' F1 – This variety turns broccoli on its head by producing plants with vivid purple stems and green heads – the total opposite to any other broccoli. This breeding breakthrough has resulted in stems that are packed with anthocyanins, resulting in the deep pigmentation that remains, getting darker as they are cooked. Attractive and delicious, this stem broccoli looks amazing.

◄ Top: 'Santee' F1; Centre: developing florets; Bottom: 'Hirzia' F1

Sprouting broccoli

'Burbank' F1 – The first British-bred, white sprouting broccoli with green stems. This unusual take on sprouting broccoli will crop from late winter for several weeks – perfect to fill the 'hungry gap' in the garden when there aren't many veggies to harvest. While it may resemble mini cauliflowers, 'Burbank' has a deliciously delicate broccoli flavour and can be used just like its purple-headed cousin.

'Santee' F1 – This may look like a traditional purple sprouting broccoli that takes almost a year to crop, yet it's a fast-growing, dual-purpose variety that is one of the most versatile you can grow; it can be sown in late winter–late spring for harvest between mid-summer and late autumn, or sow it in early summer, plant in mid-summer and harvest the following spring. The spears are tender, sweet and produced in profusion.

'Nine Star' (perennial) – This unusual broccoli looks more like a cauliflower, with smaller, tennis-ball-sized heads. Named because it can produce around nine heads, the plant produces one larger, creamy-white head, followed by smaller ones around it. Plants can be kept for over five years by preventing them from setting seed, which is simply done by harvesting all the heads before they can flower. Plants can grow larger, up to a square metre, so they should be reduced in size once all the heads have been harvested, allowing the plant to re-grow and produce more the following year. If you have the space, this is a handy plant to have in the garden, as it needs little care apart from pest prevention.

Top Tip

- Harvest the central head on stem broccoli when it is tight if you want a 'regular' broccoli, or leave it to open up and harvest as tender stem spears.

Problems (All)

Insects are the biggest problem for gardeners, ranging from cabbage root fly and butterflies to flea beetles and slugs. The easiest way to keep the flying insects off your plants is to cover them in fine-mesh insect netting as soon as they have been planted out. You can buy DIY cages to make, or simply drape the mesh over the plants and weigh it down at the side with bricks.

Mealy cabbage aphid can be a particular problem, with the whitish-coloured insects causing the leaves of your plants to curl over to protect them. Covering plants with netting will help, as will spraying affected plants with horticultural soap or SB Plant Invigorator spray; this non-toxic spray helps to get rid of pests but is safe for people and pets.

Slugs can be kept under control with beer traps or nightly inspections with a torch to pick them off your plants. It's also best to remove any debris or leaves that touch the soil, as these are all potential hiding places for slugs.

Pigeons can also be a menace to your plants, especially in the colder months when they are searching for food. Netting or mesh will keep them away if it is attached to a sturdy structure, otherwise they will land on top, then the netting sags and they eat through it!

Club root can be a problem in certain areas; this results in stunted plants with gnarled roots that don't want to grow. Adding garden lime to the soil around the planting area is reputed to help, and there's also the idea that adding a piece of rhubarb leaf to the planting hole is beneficial (I'm not sure if this is a tall tale or not, but I do it). However, to be honest there is only one thing to do if you have club root on your plot, grow club-root-resistant varieties! There are plenty on the market, so have a look for them.

◄ Top: mealy cabbage aphid;
Centre: insect-proof netting;
Bottom: pigeon damage

► Top: copper slug rings
around brassicas; Bottom:
sacrificial nasturtiums

Top Tips

- To prevent attack from cabbage white fly caterpillar, whitefly and aphids, cover your plants with a fine-mesh insect netting. This also prevents insects and hungry pigeons from getting at your plants. Sturdy supports are key, as heavy pigeons will sit on the netting to make it sag down onto the plants before they peck through to the leaves.

- Use a 'beer trap' to prevent slugs eating new seedlings. This can be as simple as a small yoghurt pot or jar half filled with beer and sunken into the soil at ground level, slugs are attracted to the beer and drown. Check daily and dispose of the slugs somewhere that birds can eat them.

- Planting nasturtiums around your plot will act as 'sacrificial' plants, attracting butterflies away from the plants you want to eat.

- Placing pots of mint around your plants will prevent insects finding them due to the strong smell – this works well for aphids, cabbage white butterflies and flea beetles. To maximise the effect, brush your hand through the mint plants every time you walk past, and it will release a minty waft!

- Using copper slug rings around newly transplanted plants will help to prevent slug and snail damage.

Onions, Garlic & Shallots

When it comes to deciding what is the most-used group of vegetables in the world, it must be the onion family (*Allium*), which includes onions, garlic, shallots and leeks. These versatile and popular vegetables are the base of almost every dish around the globe, from curries and casseroles to soups and sandwiches. We use them every day without thinking about it, often unaware of the many varieties that are available. Far from the bog-standard brown onions you can buy for pennies in the supermarket, there are pink-skinned, torpedo-shaped and even ones that are so sweet they are eaten like apples and have their own festival (see page 90)!

If you grow your own, there is a vast array of varieties available to gardeners, with onions and garlic to plant in spring or autumn, and leeks that can be harvested for months – even for years if you grow perennial ones.

One of my earliest memories of onions was in my grandad's garden. While he was weeding, I was on butterfly patrol with a small net trying to catch any cabbage white butterflies I saw. The next thing you know, five-year-old me is running through the bed of onions chasing after a butterfly while whacking all the tops of the onions over enthusiastically with the net. Needless to say, I was not the most popular helper that day!

◄ Onions ready to dry in the greenhouse

When most people think of onions they think of the brown or red-skinned ones that are sold in plastic bags in the supermarket, yet there are far more that you can grow at home.

Regardless of which you want to grow, all bulbing onions (those that produce a large bulb) are sown and grown in roughly the same way. The two main methods are using seeds or sets. Sets are small onion bulbs that will swell and create a bulb later in the year, and the advantage of these is that they are easier to grow because they need less care and attention than seeds. Growing from seed, on the other hand, gives a wider selection, and plants grown from seed are less likely to bolt before harvest. Seed-grown plants should be started in mid- to late winter as they need to be growing well before late spring; this is because the longer days trigger the plant's bulb to swell, and if your plants have more leaves by this stage, they will produce bigger and better bulbs.

How to grow

The secret to growing onions starts with the soil. You want a fertile, nutrient-rich patch in which to grow your plants and I always add a bucket of well-rotted manure or compost to each square metre of bed that I'm growing in to improve the growing conditions and hold moisture.

You can sow onion seeds into modules or directly into the ground; start module-grown plants in a greenhouse or on a windowsill at around 10–15°C (50–59°F). I like to sow 5–6 seeds per cell around 1cm (½in) deep, thinning them down to 3–4 plants as they grow, then they can either be planted as a clump or separated and planted 10cm (4in) apart to grow on. If you want smaller bulbs, you can plant them 5cm (2in) apart, resulting in more numerous, but smaller, bulbs. However, make sure you can get a small hoe in between your plants to weed them, otherwise you will have to do this by hand and it's a killer on your back; onions really don't like competition from weeds.

A faster way to grow your onions is from sets. These immature bulbs can be planted in autumn or spring, depending on the variety, and should be planted so that the pointed tip of the set is just sticking out of the soil. Always make a hole for the set with your finger or a dibber, never push it into the soil to plant it, as this can damage the basal plate, which can cause the set to rot in the ground. Again, you want to make sure your plants are between 5 and 10cm (2 and 4in) apart, dependent on the size of bulb you want, with 30cm (12in) between rows. This will allow space for you to get between your plants to weed; any closer and you risk standing on your onions. Autumn-planted sets will appreciate a nitrogen-rich feed in late winter, as this encourages growth and can help prevent the plants bolting. You can use dried chicken manure pellets or sulphate of ammonia for this, as both will do the job.

◄ 'Pink Panther'

Harvesting and storing

You'll know when your onions are ready to harvest as the leaves will start to go yellow and fall over, which means you need to check the weather forecast for a warm, dry day. Lift the onions with a fork to release the roots, taking care not to damage them as this will result in the bulb rotting quickly. Next, leave them on top of the soil to dry for a day or two before brushing the soil from the roots, then hang them upside down on wires or racks to cure and dry in the sun. If the weather is a little wet, you can dry your onions in crates in a greenhouse or well-ventilated shed until the skin is papery and the leaves become brown and dry. You can then bag up your onions for storage or braid them into strings, but whichever you do, keep them somewhere well-ventilated, cool, dry and light – storing them in the dark will encourage them to sprout.

Autumn-planted sets will be the first to harvest in mid-summer, while spring-planted and sown will be ready in late summer to early autumn. It's also worth noting that onions grown from sets usually need eating up before seed-grown varieties.

Onions to grow

White onions
'Walla Walla' – A super-sweet onion that travelled from Corsica to the USA. It's reputed to be sweet enough to eat like an apple and has its own festival to celebrate it in America. This onion is so sweet because it has less sulphur in it than other types, meaning it's also better to slice as it won't make your eyes water. Delicious in salads, sandwiches and in French onion soup, the only downside to this variety is the fact that it doesn't store for that long, so enjoy it fresh.

'Galactus' – This is a whopping onion of giant proportions, perfect for those who want an onion to enter the village show, or for those who use lots of onion in the kitchen. Found in a Scottish seed vault, this super-sized onion is easy to grow and becomes large with hardly any effort.

'White Star' F1 – A white bulbing onion that will produce a typical bulb later in the year but can also be grown to produce golf-ball-sized salad onions like the ones you find in markets in France or Italy. Make a couple of sowings and you'll have smaller ones for salads and bulbs for storing, all from the same seed packet.

Red onions
'Red Rover' – A variety that was bred for flavour and long-term storage, making it great to grow at home as it will last for months. In fact, it can be harvested in late summer and will keep well in a frost-free place until early the next summer, with some storing until mid-summer – that's almost a year!

'Pink Panther' – A highly sought-after, pink-fleshed French variety that develops a pink/coppery skin and has a mild-sweet flavour which is exceptional, especially in salads and sandwiches. The bottoms of the onions are flatter than most and they store well throughout winter.

'Karminka' – An elliptical-shaped onion, meaning it's more of a rugby ball shape. These longer bulbs are perfect for cutting in the kitchen as they don't slip or slide like round onions can. It also means they are easier to peel and prepare compared to other onions, perfect for those who use lots of onions as it saves time and effort.

▼ Harvesting 'White Star' F1

Top Tips

- Allium leaf miner is becoming more of a problem for members of the onion family, so if you see tell-tale damage of lines of white dots or small brown larvae on the leaves of your onions, you will need to lift and eat them quickly before they rot prematurely. You will also need to cover the bed with fine-mesh insect netting next year to keep the flies away.

- Blackbirds can tug your newly planted sets out of the ground thinking they are worms, so it's a good idea to place a piece of butterfly netting or horticultural fleece over the sets straight after planting until they have rooted into the soil. If not, you will be constantly replanting them.

Spring Onions

Spring onions are a great crop to grow no matter the space you have. Perfect to grow in the ground or in containers, these salad favourites are quick and easy to raise. You can sow spring onions from early spring onwards, with some varieties even growing through winter, cropping the following spring. These slender, non-bulbing plants are easily grown from seed with little fuss at all.

How to grow

Outside, simply make a 1cm (½in) deep drill in the earth (basically a shallow groove), sprinkle seeds thinly and cover with soil. Keep the area moist and as they grow you can start to harvest your plants once they reach around 15cm (6in) tall. You can also multi-sow seeds 3–5 per module and grow your plants in a greenhouse or on a sunny windowsill until they are large enough to plant out. This method allows you to grow a cluster of plants rather than a row, perfect to dot around in between slower-growing veg to get a double harvest from one space.

'White Lisbon' are the most popular to grow at home, yet there are some fantastic red and purple varieties you can grow to add colour to your salads – plus they look amazing when growing in the garden.

Harvesting and storing

Spring onions can be pulled when they are the size you require; simply loosen the soil around the base of the plant with a hand fork, pulling the plant at the same time. Spring onions can be stored in the fridge in a tall glass with 2cm (¾in) water in the base, which will keep them fresh for 7–10 days.

Spring onions to grow

'**Lilia**' – An Italian variety serving two purposes and offering a bold taste: it's ideal for cultivation as a salad onion, featuring attractive dark green leaves and a glossy, deep-red inner core; and it can be grown as a maincrop storage bulb onion, which reveals its striking red and white inner rings when mature.

'**Purplette**' – Produces small, continental-type salad onions with a purple bulb that are ideal for use raw or pickled for a different-looking pickled onion. This onion is also well suited to cooking, especially added whole into casseroles and stews.

'**Welsh Onions**' (perennial) – Looking like a typical white spring onion, this plant is a perennial variety that will come back each year and give you lots of spring onions to use however you like. This is a handy plant to have growing in the corner of a bed or even in a flower border, as it will produce pom-pom-shaped flower heads that are loved by the bees, while still allowing you to harvest the onions.

Top Tip

· Grow spring onions in the same bed as carrots and the strong smell of the onions will help to deter carrot root fly from your plants.

◄ Spring onions and carrots in the same bed to deter carrot fly
▶ Welsh onion flower

Shallots

While they may look like small onions, I like to think of shallots as the posh little cousin! Favoured by chefs and knowledgeable home cooks alike, shallots have a more refined and sweet flavour when cooked and are pretty pungent when eaten raw. I use mine not only for cooking, I also pickle them in balsamic vinegar like you would a small pickled onion, and they are sublime. You also get more for your money when growing shallots, as not only are they expensive to buy in the shops, but when you grow your own you get more than 10 bulbs for every one you plant! You can start shallots in the same way as onions, either from seed or sets; however, contrary to onions, you have more choice of varieties available to grow from sets than seeds. Shallots multiply as they grow, forming a cluster of small bulbs ranging from round to tear-drop shaped, all produced from the one set that was planted.

How to grow

Shallots need the same growing environment as onions, so be sure to add manure or compost to the beds before planting your sets. As with onions, the tip needs to be just above soil level, and you may need to net newly planted sets to protect them from the birds. The difference in growing shallots comes when you space out your plants, because they produce a wider plant than an onion, due to the bulbs multiplying. Sets should be around 15–20cm (6–8in) apart with 30–40cm (12–16in) between rows; this allows for the clump of bulbs to swell and reach around 20cm (8in) wide and still let you weed around plants effectively. There are both autumn and spring planting varieties available, so make sure you check which you are buying as some are hardier than others.

Harvesting and storing

Your shallots will be ready to harvest when the leaves begin to go yellow and flop; however, don't be tempted to pull the plants by their leaves as this can damage them. Using a garden fork, you want to lever the whole clump from the ground on a sunny day, remove as much soil as you can, and then carefully separate the bulbs without damaging them. Dry them as you would onions and they are ready to be stored until late winter or even the following spring.

Shallots to grow

'Griselle' – Known as the 'French Grey' shallot, due to the fact its skin has a grey tinge to it when it's dry and in storage. Typically known for its finer flavour and good cropping potential, this is the one I grow every year for cooking with. It's delicious!

'Jermor' – A longer, almost banana-shaped shallot, which makes it easy to prepare and slice without too much waste. This copper-skinned, French classic from Brittany also has a slight pink tinge to the flesh when peeled and it is productive, giving 7–8 bulbs back from each planted.

'Red Sun' – A round-bulbed variety with red-tinged skin and flesh, great for cooking or adding to salads, but also perfect for producing a more refined pickled onion. It's also a good size for adding whole to casseroles.

Top Tip

- There are varieties to plant in both autumn and spring, but they dislike waterlogged sites and are particularly suited to being started off in 9cm (3½in) pots in a cold frame or unheated greenhouse, then transplanted to where they will grow in spring, when the risk of cold winter rains and flooding is greatly reduced.

▼ 'Griselle'

Garlic

Perhaps one of the most rewarding onion family members to grow in the veg garden. This pungent bulb is normally used as a flavouring for other food, especially in the Mediterranean, and is recognised the world over when you see long plaits of dried bulbs hung up in homes and greengrocers. Each garlic bulb is made up of several cloves, and it's these that you plant to produce another bulb, typically starting them in the garden in autumn through to early spring. Garlic will produce the largest bulbs when planted in the open ground, but they grow well in containers, with three or four easily growing in an old bucket, as long as it has drainage holes and is watered well while the plants are growing.

There are two main types of garlic you can grow, softneck and hardneck; this refers to the stem, or 'neck', of the plant.

Hardneck
These produce bulbs with larger, more pungent-tasting cloves and when dried the plants have a hard central stem protruding from the middle of the bulb. They typically store until mid-winter. Hardneck garlic also produce flower spikes known as 'scapes'; this is the stalk that eventually produces a large, pompom-like garlic flower. Harvested before the flower opens, scapes are a real gourmet treat that you never see for sale; they have a milder, garlic-like flavour that's not overpowering, perfect for when just a hint of flavour is needed rather than a robust kick. Scapes make amazing pesto and are delicious when finely chopped and added to scrambled eggs or omelettes, or simply sautéed in butter, so don't be afraid to harvest them by grasping the plant in one hand and the scape in the other, while gently pulling until they separate.

Softneck
This garlic, on the other hand, usually produces a greater number of smaller cloves and are typically the ones you find in the supermarkets; they also keep for months longer than hardneck. Shop-bought bulbs are hardly ever produced in the UK, or even Europe; they mainly come from China, so don't be tempted to buy and grow from these as they won't be used to our cooler, wetter summers and won't produce as good a plant as one from specially produced bulbs. Growing a mix of both types will give you all the garlic you need for the year, plus a bonus crop of scapes!

Elephant
As the name suggests, elephant garlic grows to jumbo proportions and can produce enormous bulbs up to 1kg (2¼lb) in weight! It's not a true garlic, as it's related to leeks. It has a milder, sweeter taste and can be sliced thinly and added to salads without fear of overpowering the dish. Best planted in autumn to produce the largest bulbs with more cloves, it can also be planted in spring, but you run the risk of producing a monobulb (one huge, onion-like bulb), rather than it splitting into cloves. Elephant garlic can take a while to start growing and emerge from the ground, so be patient, as they will lag behind their smaller-sized cousins. Elephant garlic will also produce large scapes, so remember to harvest them, too.

How to grow

Before planting you will need to separate the cloves; this can be done by carefully peeling them apart and saving the largest to grow (as they produce the biggest bulbs). Any remaining smaller cloves can be planted in the flower border for the bees to enjoy when they flower, or you can take them into the kitchen and use them. Make sure the area is weed-free and add a bucketful of compost or well-rotted manure to every square metre of ground. Don't be tempted to push your cloves into the soil as this can damage the basal plate, which is the flat end of the clove that produces the roots. Cloves should always be planted downwards, with the pointy end at the top. When planting regular garlic, you want the tip around 2–3cm (¾–1¼in) below soil level so that the entire clove is covered, then space them 15cm (6in) apart to allow you to weed easily as they grow. Elephant garlic needs just about double the spacing and planting depth, so aim for 5–6cm (2–2½in) deep and 20–30cm (8–12in) apart, with 30cm (12in) between rows for all types.

If your site is prone to flooding, or you don't have a bed ready for your garlic in autumn, you can plant the cloves in small pots or modules, even three per old bucket (with drainage holes) and grow them on, planting out in early spring. By doing this you lessen the chance of the plant rotting in the wet and buy yourself more time to get the space ready.

Harvesting and storing

You'll know your plants are ready to harvest when the leaves start to go yellow and droop – this can be any time between late spring and late summer, depending on the variety you are growing, with softneck types sometimes going 'weak at the knees' and starting to collapse. Once this happens it's time to loosen the bulbs with a fork and leave them to dry on the soil for a day or two (weather permitting), then move them into a dry space and either space them out or hang them with the bulb facing upwards to dry. Personally, I don't plait mine as I'm not very good at it and they fall apart. Instead, I cut the stems from the semi-dry bulbs, leaving around 10cm (4in) of stalk. This allows the bulbs to dry quicker as you've taken away all the leaves and stem, then you can lay them out in trays in a single layer to fully dry. I dry elephant garlic in the same way, but after they have dried for several weeks, I split the bulbs into individual cloves to fully dry out. This is because they are so large, and they don't fully dry if left intact and can start to rot inside. By separating them, you allow them to dry out more, which in turn means they will store for longer.

Garlic to grow

'Elephant' (hardneck) – One of my favourite garlics to grow, not just because of the size, but for the milder flavour, as it works in so many dishes. Personally, I don't think you can beat roasted elephant garlic, especially mixed through pasta or rubbed over crusty bread topped with melted cheese.

'Extra Early Wight' (hardneck) – Perhaps the earliest garlic to ripen in the garden. This white-skinned variety was developed in France and has a fresh yet pungent flavour, and it also stores for months.

'Rose Wight' (hardneck) – Hailing from Northern Spain, this garlic variety boasts an beautiful outer skin in shades of rosy pink and white, with a rich, aromatic fragrance and robust, strong flavour. Best planted in autumn for a summer harvest.

'Germidour' (softneck) – This French variety has white bulbs that are flushed with purple. It has a rich yet mild flavour and is proven to grow exceptionally well in the UK – a quick grower that crops very well. A very good 'everyday' garlic.

▶ Top left: removing foliage with rust; Top right: lifting garlic to prevent damage; Centre left: removing soil from roots; Centre right: drying trimmed garlic; Bottom left: separating Elephant garlic cloves; Bottom right: Elephant garlic cloves drying

Top Tips

- Removing scapes from hardneck types not only gives you an additional harvest of garlicky goodness, it also forces the plant to concentrate its energy on producing a larger bulb rather than a flower.

- One of my favourite things to do with elephant garlic is wrap the bulb in a double layer of tin foil and bake it in the oven for an hour, or until cooked, then you can squeeze out a clove onto crusty bread for the world's best garlic bread!

- Don't leave your garlic in the ground after it's ready to harvest (especially elephant garlic), as the skin can split open and allow soil to get in between the cloves.

- The majority of garlic types need a month or two of colder winter temperatures (0–10°C/32–50°F) to force them to split into cloves, so make sure you choose the correct variety to plant in spring as opposed to planting an autumn variety.

These slender veg may be synonymous with winter food, but there are varieties that crop from autumn right the way through to late spring, with a few able to be grown as spring onions for their smaller, tender stalks in summer as well. Autumn-cropping varieties are usually faster growing and greener in colour, while winter ones are more cold-tolerant and have a blue colour to their leaves. If you want to grow leeks but don't want the hassle of sowing seeds each year, there are even perennial leeks that come back every year and will form a small colony of plants to harvest from, perfect to grow in the corner of a bed. With a more mellow taste than onions or garlic, leeks make a great base for many dishes and can be served as a vegetable; they are delicious cooked in a little butter or topped with a cheese sauce. As they are pretty cheap to buy, it's not really worth growing leeks if you have a small plot, but summer 'spring leeks' and perennial types are never seen for sale, so these types are worth growing if you can.

How to grow

For a bumper crop, add a bucket of compost or well-rotted manure per square metre of ground in autumn. You can sow seeds directly into the soil in spring; make a shallow groove around 1cm (½in) deep and water it before thinly sprinkling seed and covering. Additional rows should be 30cm (12in) apart, with plants 10–15cm (4–6in) apart when you start to thin them. As more modern F1 seed can be expensive, it may be beneficial to sow seeds in modules or a seed tray and transplant them when they are large enough to handle, 15–20cm (6–8in) tall. Leek seedlings should be 'puddled' in. This method involves creating a planting hole with a cane or dibber around 15cm (6in) deep, then you shake in all the compost from the plant and lower one seedling into each hole – the leek will look small in the deep hole, but this will encourage more white flesh as the soil will blanch it. Instead of adding soil back to the hole, water it well and the surrounding soil will collapse back into the recess without damaging the seedling, 'puddling' it back in.

You can further increase the amount of white flesh on your leeks by earthing up the plants as they grow; simply pull soil up the plants so the sun can't get to the stem, but be careful you don't get any in between the leaves as they will need serious cleaning in the kitchen if you do. Mulching around plants with well-rotted manure will help to keep plants moist, keep weeds at bay and feed your plants as they grow.

◄ Perennial 'Babington Leek'

Leeks

◄ Top left: leek seedlings; Top right: removing from seed pan; Centre left: removing compost from seedlings; Centre right: creating a hole with the dibber; Bottom left: placing seedling in a hole; Bottom right: puddling in the seedlings

Harvesting and storing

Leaving your leeks in the ground is the best option, so dig them up as and when you need them. Lift each plant with a fork to loosen the roots, then shake as much soil from the plants as you can, but do this away from the bed or you run the risk of getting it between the leaves of your remaining plants.

Leeks to grow

'Norwich' F1 – A new British-bred variety that is more rust-tolerant than most, with smooth shanks and tightly packed leaves. Plants are slow to bolt and will happily stay in the garden for weeks without splitting.

'Atal' – This is a great alternative to spring onions if you find them too hot-tasting. This mild-flavoured slender leek is quick to crop and can be grown and used in the same way as spring onions – you can even grow them in old buckets or containers. If you don't manage to eat them all while young, the plants will continue to grow and produce full-sized leeks later in the year.

'Zermatt' – A great variety to produce the smaller, 'baby' leeks you see cooked whole in fancy restaurants and for sale in expensive farm shops. A quick-growing, autumn-cropping variety that can be harvested from mid-summer when the leeks are at the size you like. Plants can also be left to mature and produce a lovely full-sized leek.

'Babington Leek' (perennial) – This slender leek with notes of garlic will come back year after year, and it's also very easy to grow and hardy. Best grown from small bulbils (tiny bulbs) and harvested by cutting the stem off at ground level, leaving the bulb to re-grow and crop again next year. Plants go dormant in the hotter summer months, disappearing back underground, only to emerge again when the cooler, damper autumn weather starts. So don't worry that you have killed them off, just try to remember where you planted them.

Top Tips

- Planting your leeks deeply will increase the amount of white flesh each plant produces.

- Producing good leeks comes down to two factors: consistent soil moisture and lots of nitrogen, so don't be shy when adding chicken manure pellets around your young plants.

All members of the onion family suffer from the same problems in the garden, with some being more serious than others.

Leek moth and allium leaf miner can damage your plants as their offspring tunnel through the plant and can cause it to rot. I've personally lost a whole harvest to the allium leaf miner before, so I now cover all my plants with fine-mesh insect netting to prevent the adults getting to the plants and laying their eggs. You should also move your plants from year to year, as crop rotation will help prevent problems building up.

Allium rust is a pathogen that creates small orange blisters on the leaves of your plants, which looks like rust. Usually more prevalent in wet summers, it's best not to crowd plants together as this increases humidity, worsening the problem. Nitrogen-rich soils can also increase the likelihood of rust, so be careful not to overfeed your plants. Any affected leaves need removing and disposing of or burning – do not compost them, as this can spread the problem. Affected plants should be harvested and used up quickly after removing affected leaves, as there is no cure and the problem will only get worse.

White rot is a fungus that produces white, cotton wool-like growths at the base of your plants, resulting in them wilting and becoming soft. It is perhaps the most serious problem for onion family members, and unfortunately there is nothing you can do but destroy the crop and clean all your tools, as this pathogen can stay dormant in the soil for several years. Don't grow anything from the onion family in that space or next to it again, as you'll suffer the same result.

◄ Harvested 'Babington Leek'

▲ Top: Insect netting to protect from leek moth and leaf miner; Bottom: allium rust

Peas, Beans, Leaves, Stems & More

Growing peas and beans at home is a sure-fire way of enjoying fresh, delicious veggies that are easy and rewarding to grow. Not only will you be harvesting baskets-full, but your garden will also be filled with many different-coloured flowers before the pods are formed, from red and white to pink, violet and even brown varieties.

One of the most significant advantages of growing these vegetables is their ability to fix nitrogen, a process that results in small white nodules developing around the roots of the plants that naturally enrich the soil and mean the plants rarely need feeding. It also promotes the growth of other plants nearby and those planted in the bed afterwards.

Typically thought of as green-podded, there are peas and beans with yellow, purple, black and even pink-flushed pods that are attractive enough to be grown in a flower border, never mind the veg patch. When it comes to size, you'll find there are plants that produce large yields while towering up canes, but only taking a small footprint of soil. Others can be grown in window boxes and baskets as they produce dwarf plants, so no matter what space you have, there's plenty of choice when it comes to growing peas and beans.

Aside from beans and peas, some vegetables have fantastically delicious stems, stalks and even cobs, yet they are rarely found in the shops, and if they are, they taste nothing like their fresh, home-grown counterparts. As you are growing these plants for the more mature parts, they need longer in the ground, with some staying there permanently and cropping year after year. Therefore, they aren't the quickest-growing or smallest plants, but they are well worth growing if you have the space.

Peas

You can quite easily buy frozen or tinned peas in the shops, yet they will taste nothing, and I mean NOTHING, like the ones you can grow at home yourself. Home-grown peas can be the sweetest, freshest vegetable you can grow; in fact, I remember walking around my grandad's garden with a fistful of pods as a child, happily munching on the sweet green peas.

When growing peas, there are a few choices to make before you start. Where are you going to grow them? The space you have for your pea plants will determine what you will be better off growing, as well as when you want to harvest. There are varieties to sow in autumn, growing through winter and cropping early in the year, which can also be grown in a greenhouse or polytunnel for an extra-early harvest; the seeds are usually smooth and round, allowing water to run around them when planted, rather than causing them to rot. Then there are spring-sown peas, which have wrinkled seeds and will crop in early summer, right the way through to the first frosts if you sow them every few weeks. There are also mangetout and sugar snap peas, all coming in a range of different colours from green to yellow, dark purple and even pink-blushed pods.

The main difference between the three types of peas is all in the pod; garden peas are shelled and the sweet peas inside are eaten, but the pods are tough and stringy even when young. Mangetout (snow peas) are grown for their edible pods, which are usually flatter, with small, immature peas inside, and they are used raw in salads or in stir-fries as they cook quickly. Sugar snaps (snap peas) have a plump, juicy pod with more-developed peas inside; they are delicious in salads and can be eaten raw or cooked. Sugar snaps are the sweetest of the three, while garden peas can be quite savoury tasting, especially if you grow the floury-textured ones, which are good for drying or making into mushy peas. The secret to producing excellent mangetout and sugar snap peas is not to allow the pods to stay on the plant and mature for too long, as some can produce a string down the length of the pod that needs removing. More modern varieties have had this bred out of them, meaning they stay tender and stringless even when large.

How to grow

If you are growing a shorter-sized variety, which grows 40–75cm (15–30in) tall, you can easily sow in a drill. Peas can be started off outside in the soil from early spring; all you need to do is create a flat-bottomed drill 15cm (6in) wide and sow your seeds in a zig-zag pattern around 5cm (2in) deep and 7–8cm (2¾–3in) apart. After covering them with soil and watering you will want to push a few twiggy sticks into the drill for the peas to hold on to with their tendrils as they grow. Subsequent rows should be planted at a distance that's the same as the height of the variety you are growing. If you are growing a taller variety that needs support, it is best to erect the wigwam or frame before sowing your seed next to the supports, making sure there is something for the emerging plant to climb up. Climbing peas are the best choice for those with smaller gardens or limited space, as you only use a small footprint for your plants, yet you'll get up to 2m (6½ft) tall towers of productive peas; you can even sow a few different colours together for an ornamental and edible display.

▶ 'Douce Provence'

Peas like a deep root run while they are growing, so you can use root-trainer trays, deep modules or toilet rolls placed in a seed tray and filled with compost; just be careful you don't water the latter too much as the cardboard can become soggy and green before the seedlings are ready to plant. Sow 2–3 seeds per roll around 5cm (2in) deep, grow on until large enough to handle, harden off and plant out where required. To save even more space, I start seeds off in terracotta bowls (old ice cream tubs with drainage holes would also work) of compost by thickly scattering them and covering with more compost. Then, when the seedlings are 10–15cm (4–6in) tall, it's easy to knock the compost from the roots and separate them, before planting out where you want them to grow, just like bare-root plants. I've used this method of planting peas for years and it works well.

You can also 'gutter sow' your seeds in an old piece of guttering in the greenhouse; this allows you to start them off under cover and simply slide the seedlings, compost and all, into a channel dug in the soil where you want them to grow. Shorter varieties can be grown with the aid of twiggy pea sticks, allowing the tendrils to hold the plants upright; you can also use pea gates to grow against or special hoop supports that hold netting for the plants to cling to.

Peas aren't just for spring sowing, there are certain varieties that can be started from autumn to early winter. I find these are best sown under cover in pots or modules and transplanted as young plants. They also need extra protection with netting, otherwise pigeons will decimate them in the colder months while they look for food. If you have an unheated greenhouse, you can grow autumn-sown peas in there, which should crop before you need the space back for tomatoes and other crops in late spring.

Harvesting and storing

When harvesting, always start at the bottom of the plant, as this is where the most mature pods will be. Using two hands, hold the plant and pod, twisting gently where you see the elbow, which connects the pod to the plant. If you find this difficult, just use a pair of flower snips to cut the pod from the plant, but never yank them as you can pull the plants up or damage the tendrils that are attached to supports.

Mangetout are the quickest pea to crop; they should be picked when you can just see the pea starting to develop in the pod and it is still flat. Sugar snaps can be harvested thinner, or left until oval-shaped, as this is when they will be at their juiciest – although don't leave them too long as you don't want them to get too stringy. Garden peas should be harvested when the peas have filled the pods but before they start to look wrinkly, as this is a sign the pea inside may be hard and starchy rather than crisp and sweet.

All peas are best used straight away or kept in the fridge for a couple of days to preserve their sweetness. Garden peas can be shelled and frozen to use later in the year, while sugar snaps and mangetout will need blanching before freezing.

Peas to grow

Garden peas
'Douce Provence' (autumn sowing) – This shorter variety (60–75cm/24–30in) is happy to grow through the winter outside, though some protection with fleece may be needed if it becomes very cold. It's one of the first to crop in spring and has deliciously sweet peas. I like to grow this in my unheated greenhouse through the winter, with the first pods harvested in early to mid-spring.

'Blauwschokker' – An old heritage variety of climbing pea, reaching around 2m (6½ft) tall. The flowers are reminiscent of sweet peas, with beautiful magenta and pink petals, followed by dark purple pods that can be harvested as mangetout or left to swell into lime-green peas. Having more of a savoury flavour, the peas make a good dip when mashed with feta, garlic and olive oil; they also dry well and can be added to winter soups and stews.

'Sabrina' – This may be a regular green garden pea, but it's perhaps the most disease-resistant variety you can grow, shrugging off both downy and powdery mildew while those around it succumb. Pods are filled with very sweet, crisp peas, and plants are very tolerant of cooler temperatures, so they are perfect for a British summer! Plants are a manageable 75cm (30in) tall, meaning they can be grown in pots as well as in the garden.

Mangetout and sugar snaps
'Spring Blush' (sugar snap) – An outstanding decorative and edible plant! It's a lofty, climbing type that requires ample support to achieve its full potential. In exchange, you'll be treated to a charming display of dual-tone pink blossoms, accompanied by an abundance of light-green pods with a hint of rosy pink. Ideal for incorporating a splash of colour to stir-fries or enjoying raw. This robust sugar snap pea variety also generates numerous tendrils that can be picked and used in salads; this 'hyper-tendril' habit also means plants climb and cling to supports very well, keeping them safe in strong winds.

'Purple Magnolia' (sugar snap) – A genuine eye-catcher in the garden, and the world's first purple sugar snap pea. It has striking deep-purple pods that create a stunning contrast with the lush green leaves. Its sweet, crunchy pods make a great addition to salads, veggie platters and stir-fries. Alternatively, the pods can be left to mature and shelled for use as peas. The robust, sturdy plants, measuring 1.8–2m (6–6½ft) in height, yield highly decorative, two-toned fuchsia and vivid purple flowers, as well as hyper-tendrils that easily attach to a fence or trellis.

'Golden Sweet' (mangetout) – Produces very distinctive golden pods on tall climbing plants that reach 1.8–2m (6–6½ft). The flowers are bicoloured and even the leaf nodes are an attractive red colour, but nothing is as attractive as the deliciously crisp pods. If you don't manage to harvest all the pods when they are thin and crisp, you can leave them to swell and produce peas for drying, which are excellent in soups.

'Snow Max' (mangetout) – A modern breeding breakthrough, producing one of the most disease-resistant mangetout peas there is. Resistant to both downy and powdery mildew, this shorter 75cm (30in) tall plant has a bushy habit with lots of tendrils, which means it almost supports itself without the need for lots of pea sticks. It's also semi-leafless, meaning it has fewer leaves, making it easier to see and harvest the sweet, crunchy pods, which are almost stringless.

Problems

Powdery mildew occurs as late summer arrives. This fungal issue is characterised by a white film that appears on the leaves and can spread throughout the entire crop. Mildew becomes more prevalent with the gradual shift in temperature as autumn approaches. You can help prevent it by making sure you give enough space between plants for good air circulation, and avoid watering the leaves, only soaking the soil. If you spot signs of mildew, you can remove affected plants or consider spraying with SB invigorator, a trusted method of control used by many professional organic growers.

Pea moth is when small caterpillars are found inside pods when you come to shell your peas. They are harmless, and undamaged surrounding peas can be eaten once washed. However, to avoid the problem you can grow your plants under fine-mesh insect netting or sow your seeds early or late so that they are not flowering in mid-summer when the moth is laying its eggs. Autumn-sown peas don't suffer and most mangetout are unaffected as you eat the pod before the pea forms.

- Protect early seedlings from hungry pigeons by covering or wrapping structures and plants in horticultural fleece to keep them out – this will also give your plants a little protection from the cold.

- Sow pea seeds every couple of weeks to ensure a constant supply of peas throughout the season

- Growing peas surrounded by copper slug rings will help prevent damage from slugs in the early stages of the plants' life.

◄ Mangetout 'Snow Max'

▲ Previous pages: Left top: sowing in a seed pan; Left centre: firming the compost; Left bottom: germinating peas; Right top: gutter sowing; Right centre: creating a trench for the gutter peas; Right bottom: sliding peas from gutter

Broad Beans

These are a low-maintenance and productive vegetable, offering valuable early yields before most other crops are harvested. Depending on your growing conditions and the variety, they can be planted from autumn to late spring, with some even being sown in summer. Hardier varieties can be planted in the autumn, while others are better suited for late winter or spring sowing. By sowing multiple batches you can enjoy fresh, tasty beans from early to late summer, even into autumn. These beans prefer a sunny, protected location with rich, well-draining soil, and compact varieties can be successfully grown in containers or small spaces.

They require very little care, just occasional weeding and watering during dry periods once flowering begins, then frequent harvesting as pods develop to promote continued production. There is a wide range of broad bean varieties, each with unique planting and harvesting times, plant heights and pod sizes; they also come with different-coloured edible flowers and some can even be eaten whole like a mangetout. Some grow to hip height, while others only get to around 30cm (12in) tall. In the kitchen, broad beans can be podded young and simply enjoyed for the sweet, tasty bean; older pods can be podded, then the skin of the bean removed, and these 'double-podded' beans make a delicious dip, or can be frozen for later use in soups, casseroles and stews.

How to grow

As broad beans have a large seed, they readily attract mice, which can devour them within hours of sowing. Therefore, I prefer to start my seeds under cover in an unheated greenhouse or cold frame, but you can sow them directly if mice aren't a problem for you.

Prepare the bed before sowing or planting out with a bucket of well-rotted manure per square metre, forking it in well and removing any weeds, then rake and level your soil. Seeds should be sown 5–6cm (2–2½in) deep, 15cm (6in) apart in rows, with 25–30cm (10–12in) between rows. Autumn-sown seeds will need some protection with a cloche or fleece, which prevents new growth from frost damage if a hard or prolonged frost is experienced; broad beans are hardy enough to survive light frost easily.

If you would prefer to start seeds off under cover, it's best to use a deep module, toilet roll or other container that can accommodate the plants' large roots. Sow the seeds around 5cm (2in) deep, water the modules and leave them somewhere cool but protected, such as a cold frame or unheated greenhouse – you don't want to give them extra heat as then they will produce tall and leggy seedlings. Once your plants reach around 10cm (4in) tall they can be hardened off and planted out in their final growing positions if the soil is not frozen or waterlogged.

Taller varieties will benefit from some support as they reach their final height, with a 'boxing ring'-type structure working well. I push a stout pole into all four corners of the bed, then tie thin rope around them at 30cm (12in) and 60cm (24in) from the ground, which helps support the plants as they produce heavy pods, and stops them from falling over in spring gales.

▶ 'Aquadulce Claudia'

Short varieties can be grown successfully in large containers at least 40cm (16in) wide, just make sure your plants are 15cm (6in) apart, ideally. Water container-grown plants well and don't let them dry out, as this can affect their yield.

Once your plants have produced their first small pods towards the base of the plant, it's time to remove the growing tip with a sharp pair of secateurs. By doing this you will force the plant to concentrate on producing larger pods, but it will also remove the soft growing tip, which would otherwise encourage blackfly to your plants.

Harvesting and storing

Using a pair of secateurs, harvest pods from the base of the plant, working your way upwards. Small pods less than 7cm (2¾in) long can be cooked whole and eaten like mangetout, whereas larger ones should be harvested when you can feel the bean but it's not too large, otherwise it will be tough.

You can store pods in a plastic bag in the fridge for a couple of days before podding, but the sooner you pod them, the better. Once you have your beans, I like to use the small ones in salads, whereas the larger ones need blanching. To blanch broad beans before freezing, fill a large pan with water and bring it to a rolling boil, while also preparing an ice bath in a separate large bowl. Add the podded beans to the boiling water, and blanch for 1–2 minutes, depending on their size. Then use a slotted spoon or strainer to transfer the beans to the ice bath, where they should be allowed to cool completely. This process ensures the beans keep their flavour, texture and nutrients before freezing. Once completely dry, bag them up and pop them in the freezer for later use.

Broad beans to grow

'Crimson Flowered' – A heritage variety of broad bean known for its striking deep-red flowers. These plants produce long, slender pods containing tender beans, which have a delicious flavour when picked young. If you don't have much space in the garden these will blend in if grown in a flower border, as the flowers look like red orchid blooms.

◄ Top: Tunnel cloche over plants; Centre: Creating 'boxing ring' support; Bottom: tender bean (green scar), tough bean (dark scar)

'Mr Grief's Brown Flowered' – Another heritage broad bean with chocolate-brown flowers, producing short pods with 4–5 beans in each. This variety is extremely rare and hard to get hold of, but well worth growing if you can find it.

'The Sutton' – A short 30–40cm (12–16in) tall plant, which produces masses of beans. It's suited to growing in the ground, raised beds and containers, making it perfect for those with limited space. Easy to grow and productive, this variety is great for those taking their first steps in gardening.

'Luz de Otono' – This is a broad bean lover's dream, being the world's first autumn-cropping variety. This means you'll not only be harvesting in late spring/ summer, but into autumn as well! Sown in late summer, this speedy variety will crop in late autumn, but will need a little protection with fleece if the weather is predicted to be very cold.

Problems

Blackfly are a notorious pest on broad beans, concentrating on the growing tips in summer. I find the easiest way to avoid them is to remove the soft growing tips that the pests like to feed on at the first sign of them, or even better you can cut the tops off your plants as soon as the first pod has set.

Bean weevil are small beetle-like insects that remove a tell-tale notch from the edge of your plants' leaves. This isn't a problem for mature plants as they can grow through any damage, but it can slow the growth on small seedlings if they are affected. Starting seeds under cover and planting them out when they are growing strongly will help them cope better. Growing under fleece or cloches can help prevent much damage. The adult beetles overwinter in leaf litter, so keeping your plot tidy and growing your plants in different beds each year will help to prevent an infestation.

Chocolate spot and rust both produce brown spots on the plants' leaves that can spread and become larger in wet weather. They don't usually affect your harvest unless severe chocolate spot causes the stems of plants to collapse. Giving plants plenty of space between them can help increase airflow and reduce the risk of these problems arising. Any affected plants should be destroyed or added to domestic waste, not composted.

Top Tips

- If sowing directly into the ground, sow a few extra seeds at either end of the row, as there are always one or two that won't germinate, so these spares can fill in any gaps.

- During cold weather or frost, you may notice your plants look as if they have collapsed or sagged – this is perfectly normal, and you should leave them to defrost and perk up on their own. Don't be tempted to try to stand them back up as this can damage or snap the stems.

- Module-sown seeds can be placed in a tray on an upside down bucket, which will prevent mice getting to the seeds.

- The tops of broad bean plants can be eaten like cabbage, either steamed or added to stir-fries. With a delicious bean-like taste, this bonus crop is only available if you grow your own!

- When removing beans from mature pods, make sure the scar where a bean was attached to the pod is light in colour, as this ensures it will be tender and sweet. If it's dark brown or black, the bean will be tough and starchy.

Runner beans are a classic staple in kitchen gardens and can be found on allotments and vegetable patches throughout the country. Initially cultivated as ornamental plants in Britain, they continue to be admired for their vivid, eye-catching flowers. While traditional varieties produce scarlet blooms, contemporary cultivars offer white, bicoloured and pink-peach flowers that gracefully twine around bamboo canes. Alongside varying flower colours, there are also varieties with unique pod hues, including deep purple or nearly black pods that have gained popularity in recent times. Contrary to the common belief that runner beans grow exclusively as tall climbers, dwarf varieties can be successfully grown in containers, pots or even baskets, making them a versatile addition to any garden space. Enjoyed fresh during the summer season, runner beans can also be frozen for later use, while their seeds can be dried and stored for years, making them a valuable ingredient in winter dishes like casseroles, soups and chillies. Some large, white-seeded varieties can even serve as a substitute for butter beans.

Modern breeding has introduced not only stringless runner beans but also 'super-runners', a clever crossbreed of runner and French beans. This innovative variety is self-fertile, ensuring a bountiful harvest even in poor weather conditions or when pollinators like bees are scarce, unlike traditional runner beans, which may drop their flowers and produce a smaller crop.

How to grow

Runner beans flourish in sunny but sheltered locations. Before planting, clear the area of weeds and mix in a generous amount of well-rotted manure or garden compost – approximately two bucketsful per square metre. Ideally, do this several weeks in advance or even the previous autumn to allow the soil to settle. Runner beans are climbing plants and so need tall supports. While they are traditionally grown along rows of tall bamboo canes, wigwams or bean towers can also be used, adding height and variety in the garden. You can even buy tower composters that fit inside, allowing you to grow and add more compost at the same time. Wigwams are particularly suitable for smaller gardens with limited space.

Seeds can be sown 5cm (2in) deep in pots, deep modules or root trainers and placed on a sunny windowsill or in a heated greenhouse propagator. Avoid starting seeds too early, as they should not be planted outdoors until the risk of frost has passed. To protect the seeds from mice, place the tray of newly sown seeds on an upturned bucket to prevent the mice reaching them. You can wait until late spring to sow seeds indoors if you are not growing them in a polytunnel. By the time the plants reach about 30cm (12in) tall, they can be hardened off for 10–14 days and then planted directly in the garden. Alternatively, you can sow seeds outside by their supports once the soil has warmed – typically around late spring to early summer. Sow two seeds per cane and thin to the strongest seedling. Runner beans love damp, cool summers, making them a good choice for most gardens in the UK.

◄ 'Black Knight'

Runner Beans

Harvesting and storing

As your plants begin to produce crops, picking ripe pods can become a daily task. These prolific plants can generate a large number of beans, and it's essential to harvest them while they're tender and juicy, even if you have to share the surplus. This approach ensures that the plants continue to produce more pods instead of focusing their energy on maturing the seeds inside. It's recommended to use scissors or secateurs to remove the beans from the plant to prevent any damage.

Fresh pods can be stored in the refrigerator for 5–7 days before they start to soften, but you can also freeze runner beans with ease. Blanch them in boiling water for a minute or two, then immerse them in an ice bath until cooled. Allow them to dry before freezing. If you prefer using the seeds as dry beans, let the pods remain on the plants until they begin to dry. Then remove them and place them in a cool, dry area to dry out completely. The seeds will effortlessly pop out of the hard, dry pods, and after a few more days, to reduce the water content in the seed, they can be stored in glass jars in a cupboard.

Runner beans to grow

'Firestorm' – This is a 'super-runner', a self-pollinating cross of runner and French beans, that ensures a consistent crop regardless of weather conditions or pollinator visits. Boasting eye-catching bright red flowers, this variety produces entirely stringless pods with an exceptional taste.

'Black Knight' – This red-flowered runner bean actually has dark purple, almost black pods, and is said to have been grown by the Bishop of Shrewsbury, Edmund Knight, and shared with some local congregants in the late 1800s. The origin of this story may be rooted in truth or simply be a folktale, as its actual source has been lost to time and history. The beans of 'Black Knight' might appear somewhat more rugged than others, but they remain tender and juicy even as the pods age and the beans become more visible. It is best to steam the beans lightly, preserving some of their colour and keeping their excellent flavour.

'Czar' – A versatile runner bean that serves a dual purpose. It produces tender, succulent pods from white flowers, followed by sizeable white seeds that can be dried and used like butter beans. This variety is ideal for gardeners who may not have the time to harvest their plants daily because the more mature pods can be left to yield home-grown butter beans.

'Jackpot Mixed' – A dwarf runner bean variety that yields an abundance of full-sized beans from plants reaching just 50cm (20in) in height. Additionally, it is a hybrid with French beans, making the plant self-fertile and capable of producing a crop regardless of weather conditions, while also offering stringless pods. Its compact size makes it perfect for growing in pots, containers or even large hanging baskets, allowing you to grow runner beans even in limited garden spaces.

Problems

Pod-setting failure can be a concern with runner beans, particularly during hot summers. Insufficient watering may cause plants to shed their flowers before pod formation begins. To address this, it is advisable to enrich the soil with ample organic matter where the plants will grow and apply mulch around them to help retain moisture. Ensure that the plants are watered adequately during dry periods, but avoid misting the flowers, as this outdated advice has not proven effective in enhancing pod-setting.

◄ Top: immature runner bean seeds; Bottom: 'Black Knight'
▼ Dried runner bean seeds, ready to cook

- Always erect supports for bean plants before sowing them directly or planting out; this avoids any damage to seedlings and allows them to begin climbing straight away.

- Create a pit or trench in late winter where your plants are going to grow, then fill this with kitchen waste over several months before covering with soil and leaving to settle. This organic-rich growing area will be the perfect place to grow beans, as they are hungry plants, requiring good soil and lots of moisture. Alternatively, you can also use a tower composter which allows you to carry on composting as plants cover the surrounding structure.

- If you happen to overlook harvesting and find yourself with a large yield of mature, inedible bean pods, there's no need to worry. The fully grown beans inside the pods can be utilised in cooking just like haricot beans, making them perfect for warming winter soups and casseroles.

- When assisting a wayward plant in locating its support to climb, keep in mind that runner beans twirl clockwise around a cane, meaning they progress from left to right when observed head-on. Forcing them to grow in the opposite direction will cause them to unwind overnight.

French Beans

In the UK, we commonly call them French beans, but around the world they're known as pole beans, bush beans, green beans, string beans and snap beans. This is likely because these beans became popular in France before spreading to other countries, including the UK.

Arguably the most sophisticated bean you can grow in your garden, they're typically consumed before the seed inside matures, offering a distinct tenderness and delicate, sweet taste that pairs well with a variety of dishes – from salads and stir-fries to simply steamed or sautéed as a side dish. While green beans are most common, you'll also find yellow, purple and even pink-red varieties, some with round, pencil-like pods and others with flatter, runner bean-like shapes. One of the great advantages of French beans is their self-pollinating nature, ensuring a steady crop regardless of weather conditions or insect visits. This makes them perfect for growing in hotter, drier years since, unlike runner beans, French beans won't drop their flowers and will continue to crop.

With heights ranging from 40cm (16in) to 2m (6¹/₂ft), French beans can be grown in almost any space – from window boxes and pots to raised beds and open gardens. Additionally, these plants help convert atmospheric nitrogen, nourishing nearby plants. This makes them perfect for growing alongside other plants requiring extra nutrients, like corn or kale. I love planting dwarf French beans around my sweetcorn, as it allows me to harvest two crops from the same area while boosting the corn yield simultaneously.

Climbing beans will produce a great crop in a space with a small footprint, while dwarf beans are very quick to grow and crop, benefiting from several sowings over the season to ensure a constant harvest.

How to grow

Regardless of whether you are growing climbing or dwarf French beans, how you sow them is the same. You can start seed off either indoors or outside, but you will need to wait for the soil temperatures to warm up before sowing directly; while you are waiting, you can sow your first batch of beans on a windowsill to give you a head start. Using small pots, modules or old toilet rolls, sow two seeds each around 5cm (2in) deep and keep the compost moist (not wet) and warm, then remove the weakest seedling as they germinate. Don't be tempted to start seeds too early as they grow quickly, so mid-spring is ideal – any earlier and your plants could be leggy and weak before they can be planted out.

After all chance of frost has passed, start hardening off plants by leaving them outside in the day and bringing them back in at night for 7–10 days before planting them out, either around their supports if they are climbing varieties, or straight into their beds or containers if they are dwarf types; both should be 15cm (6in) apart. Some of the older dwarf varieties may benefit from having a few twiggy sticks inserted into the row to add support as the pods are produced, which prevents them resting on the soil; modern varieties normally produce their pods above the leaves to make harvesting easier. Planting dwarf beans in blocks rather than rows helps them support each other as they grow – just make sure the block isn't too big, as you need to be able to reach the middle from all sides. Alternatively, plant your dwarf beans at the edge of

► 'Adoration', 'Celine' and 'Compass'

raised beds and allow them to hang over the edge, which makes harvesting a doddle.

Climbing varieties can be grown up wigwams or rows of canes in the veg garden or in the flower border to provide interest and colour; they look particularly good when green, yellow and purple pods are grown together. When plants reach the top of their supports, snip off the growing tip and let it concentrate on producing beans rather than growing skyward, otherwise the tips can tangle into a knot of plants. Plants can become heavy when laden with beans, so make sure your structures are sturdy.

You can sow French beans outside until early summer and still get a decent crop, especially if growing a quick-cropping climbing or dwarf variety. Remember to water plants well as they can be thirsty when the pods are forming, especially if it's a hot year. Mulching around the plants with compost or well-rotted manure in early summer can help to prevent water evaporation and keep them moist.

Harvesting and storing

Once pods are large enough to harvest, it's time to get picking! Make sure you keep picking pods before the seeds inside begin to swell, as this will ensure your plants keep cropping for longer, with dwarf varieties producing for several weeks and climbing ones for much longer. You should be able to easily snap beans from the plant, but it's worth having a pair of snips to hand to help with any stubborn pods. Be careful not to pull dwarf plants from the ground when harvesting – cutting one pod at a time is preferable to pulling a cluster all at once.

Beans should be harvested from your plants when they are ready, even if you don't need them yet, which ensures more are produced and plants don't use their energy to ripen the seeds inside the pods, otherwise they go tough. You can blanch and freeze excess beans or keep them in a plastic bag in the fridge with a piece of damp kitchen paper, which will keep them fresh for around a week without them going soft.

French beans to grow

Dwarf varieties
'Adoration' (yellow) – This attractive, glossy yellow bean is exceptionally slender and straight, making it ideal for incorporating into salads or serving as a standalone side dish. Reaching a height of approx. 45cm (18in), it is well-suited to growing in pots and containers, as well as directly in the garden.

'Celine' (purple) – Selected by the breeder from over 50 potential varieties, this extra-fine purple bean has a nuttier flavour than most and boasts beautiful purple and white bicoloured flowers before the beans are produced.

'Red Swan' (flat red) – This appealing, rosy red bean is a true attention-grabber, adding visual interest to pots and containers while also making the beans more visible and faster to pick. The plants display lovely pink flowers preceding the production of stringless, 8–15cm (3–6in) beans. To maintain some of their vibrant colour, add these beans to a stir-fry just before serving, as boiling will result in them losing colour and turning green.

'Compass' (green) – Although this is a standard green colour, this bean has a fantastic flavour and very fine pods, making it far superior to those you buy in the supermarket. If you want to grow a traditional green variety, this is the one to go for.

'Atlanta' (flat green) – Unusually for dwarf beans, this Romano (or Italian flat bean) has flat pods almost like a smooth runner bean. Stringless, with a great flavour, this bean is compact and quick to grow, making it one of the first to crop and last to so later in the season, enabling you to keep cropping for longer. Shorter, 40cm (16in) tall plants are great for containers and even window boxes.

Climbing varieties
'Carminat' (purple) – An extremely productive and easy-to-see bean, which makes it a doddle to harvest without missing a pod. The slender, deep-purple pods are produced in clusters, making it an attractive plant in the flower borders as well as the veg patch. Perfect to grow up a wigwam.

'Sunshine' (yellow) – Producing pods up to 18cm (7in) long, this sunshine-yellow bean is stringless and very tasty, plus it has slender, juicy pods. Keep picking this productive variety and it will crop up until the first frost, meaning you'll get four months of beans from your plants.

'Cobra' (green) – A traditional green climbing bean which produces masses of pods, perfect to grow along with your coloured climbing beans. It's a vigorous climber and starts cropping quickly, so make sure you provide a strong structure for your plants.

▼ 'Sunshine' and 'Carminat'

Top Tips

· Growing nasturtiums around the base of French beans can attract blackfly away from the tender growing tips, allowing you to simply compost the nasturtium plants when they become infested.

· Growing lettuce in the shade created by climbing beans will prevent them from bolting as quickly in hot weather, allowing you to harvest for longer.

· Water the soil around the plants, not the leaves, as this ensures every bit of water gets to the roots rather than staying on the plants, where it can scorch them in sunny weather.

· When your plants have finished cropping, cut them off at ground level and compost the top. Leave the roots in the ground to allow the following crop to access the nitrogen-rich nodules on the plant's roots.

· Growing dwarf beans around the base of corn or kale can help feed the other crop, resulting in larger harvests from the taller plants.

· Purple beans will change to green if boiled for any length of time; try lightly steaming or stir-frying them to retain some colour.

· Try mixing two or three different-coloured beans together and sowing them, in this way you'll be rewarded with a kaleidoscope of colour when it comes to harvest time.

These must be the quickest, easiest and most versatile leaves you can grow, with the most popular and well known for salads and sandwiches being the lettuce. Speciality leaves are expensive in the supermarket, with a gas-filled bag of leaves only lasting a couple of meals if you're lucky, yet you can grow your own and have a variety of colours, textures and flavours all season long. Plants are easy to grow in any container, from pots and trays to borders and raised beds; in fact, they can be started any time of year for a constant supply of fresh leaves on your windowsill. By growing these quick-cropping veggies you can really maximise your space, filling it with expensive to buy, easy to grow crops.

Lettuce ranges from crisphead to butterhead, romaine/cos, batavia and cut-and-come-again varieties, with many colours and patterns as well as leaf shapes. Mainly thought of as a salad ingredient, you can add lettuce to sandwiches and stir-fries and even griddle or barbecue them.

How to grow

All lettuce seed is started in the same way – either sown direct into the garden or container where they are to grow and be harvested, or started off in modules and planted out into the garden where you like. Sowing direct into the garden couldn't be easier. If you want to grow a full lettuce like an iceberg, simply sow the seed thinly in a line, cover with a thin layer of soil and keep moist. As the seedlings grow, you'll need to thin them out to 15–20cm (6–8in), using the thinned plants in salads or transplanting them elsewhere in the garden. If you are growing a cut-and-come-again mix which you are going to harvest as young leaves, scatter the seed where it is to grow (container, bed or border) and allow to germinate and form a solid bed of leaves. These leaves are harvested by 'tipping' them, meaning they are cut when they reach 10–15cm (4–6in) tall. If you leave 2–3cm (¾–1¼in) at the base of the plant, they should regrow and allow you to take another harvest in a few weeks' time.

Starting plants in small modules involves sowing 2–4 seeds per cell, to allow for any germination failures. As they grow, thin the plants to the best one and allow to grow on until the roots start to protrude from the base of the module. Then you can either pot them up into individual pots or transplant into the garden where they are to crop.

Salad leaves to grow

Growing a mix of varieties, colours and textures is easy and much cheaper than buying bagged lettuce all year, especially if you buy a ready-made mixed packet of seed. You can then grow them as cut-and-come-again lettuces or sow a few seeds to produce larger plants to add to the veg patch.

Crispheads

Known as icebergs in the shops, these form a dense, ball-shaped plant which is perfect for a crisp texture. But why stick to pale green when growing at home? There is a beautiful red-tinged variety called 'Red Iceberg', which adds interest to both the garden and your plate, and there are other varieties, such as 'Warpath' and 'Sweet Success', which are crispheads crossed with romaine types, producing sweet, crispy leaves with a darker green colour. Crispheads are less prone to bolting (flowering and going to seed) than most other types. If you want to grow a crispy, slightly bitter salad leaf through winter in an unheated greenhouse, you can't go wrong with 'Frillice'; it's a cross between an iceberg and endive, resulting in lime-green, frilly leaves with a good crunch and flavour. Seeds can be sown in mid autumn and will grow slowly, giving cut-and-come-again leaves all winter and into spring.

Romaine/cos

These lettuces are the same thing, it just depends on where you come from as to what you know them as. In the US they are typically called romaine, while they are called cos in the UK. Crunchy with a thick midrib, the plants stand upright and have a more oblong shape. Most varieties are a darker green colour, yet there are a few with extremely deep-red colouration, such as 'Amaze', 'Volcana' and 'Outredgeous', which was the first plant grown from seed and eaten on the International Space Station, thanks to the fact that it can grow in lower-light conditions. There are even varieties such as 'Freckles' and 'Speckled Trout' that have red splotches and speckles on the green leaf, giving rise to their names. 'Little Gem' is also a smaller-sized cos, which has gained popularity up and down the country for its flavour and how easy it is to grow, and 'Winter Density' is a cos you can grow through winter.

Butterhead

These types have a more relaxed, open shape with softer, more 'buttery' textured leaves. They will tolerate poorer soil conditions, and certain varieties are less affected by the heat, while others such as 'Arctic King' and 'Brighton' can be grown through the winter months, cropping in spring. There are also red-flushed 'Roxy' and 'Marvel of Four Seasons', which has attractive red-bronze tips and has been grown by avid gardeners since the 1800s.

Batavia

A loose-leaf type of lettuce that has crisp leaves like a cos but with the more open habit of a butterhead, allowing single leaves to be harvested – perfect for when you only need a few leaves. They don't bolt and set seed easily and are more drought-resistant than other types of lettuce, so they are easier to grow, with leaves that range from slightly crinkled to extremely curly. 'Tarengo' forms rosettes of loose leaves with a red-tinted, slightly glossy leaf, while the more traditional 'Blonde de Paris' has crisp, sweet green leaves almost like an iceberg. 'Grewger' (aka 'Burger Leaf') forms rounded leaves which are the perfect shape to add to a burger, and they stay crisp even when hot; perfect for harvesting one leaf at a time.

Loose-leaf

These lettuces are varieties that don't form a solid head, but instead they produce a rosette of leaves in differing shapes and colours. When harvesting, you can either pick the leaves a few at a time to allow longer cropping, or you can make one cut at the base and harvest the entire plant. When harvested like this the leaves separate and are easier to wash and prepare. The most popular varieties are 'Salad Bowl Green' and 'Salad Bowl Red', as they literally fill a salad bowl when harvested as a whole plant. Grown together, they produce a ready-made mix that will crop for several weeks and is slow to bolt. One of the most modern and darkest-leaved lettuces must be 'Oakus', with deep purple, almost black oak-shaped leaves with a lime-green centre, perfect to add interest to salads.

Rocket (Arugula)

This makes a great salad leaf; its peppery flavour and crisp texture means it is a good addition to any mixed salad. You can grow wild or garden rocket, with the former generally being a perennial plant that will come back the following year if given some winter protection, while the latter is classed as an annual. With the addition of rocket leaves in bagged salad mixes, the number of varieties has increased dramatically. Most gardeners grow rocket as an annual and make multiple sowings throughout the season, with some preferring the slender, deeply divided leaves of the wild types, and others opting for the rounded, milder-tasting salad rocket. Rocket by name, rocket by nature! Not only are most varieties quick to germinate and grow, but they can also be fast to flower, which in turn increases the pungency of the leaves. You can get around this by sowing a pinch of seeds every few weeks, giving a continuous supply of leaves; but don't let the yellow flowers go to waste, as they make a great addition to salads or a garnish for soups.

If you like your rocket to be hot and spicy, 'Wildfire' is a wild type with extremely peppery and tangy leaves and an upright habit, so it's perfect to grow in pots or the ground as it won't flop and rot on the soil. If you're after a unique-looking variety, try 'Dragon's Tongue', as this is a slow-to-bolt wild type that has a gorgeous purple veining to the leaves, great for adding colour and pungency to salads. For a totally different taste you could grow 'Wasabi' rocket. Unlike its namesake, which is a root, 'Wasabi' rocket produces masses of green leaves with the flavour of wasabi or horseradish, and is great served with sushi or seafood.

▶ Harvesting 'Frillice' during the winter

Sown and grown in almost the same way as lettuce, rocket seeds are small, so be careful how many you sow as a pinch goes a long way. Rocket is a handy veg to grow in an unheated greenhouse throughout the winter months. It can be started off after you remove your tomatoes, allowing you to harvest it from baby leaf stage to mature plants in spring. As the weather warms up the plants will start to flower, but that's about the time you'd be thinking to clear the beds and prepare for the return of tomato plants, so it's a perfect plant to fill that empty gap.

Land cress

You may remember eggshells as a child when you think of cress, but land cress (aka American cress) couldn't be further from the truth; in fact, it's got more in common with watercress! Watercress is not only expensive to buy, with it being in season for a short time in the UK, but it's also very demanding to grow in the garden as ideally you need running water. Land cress, on the other hand, will grow in any moisture-retentive, partly shaded area of the garden, even in containers. Looking very similar and tasting almost identical to its aquatic counterpart, land cress can crop in as little as 8–10 weeks from sowing, making it an ideal component in salads and sandwiches. Seeds can be started in the open or in modules, sowing them around 0.5cm (¼in) deep, then once plants are large enough to handle they should be placed 20cm (8in) apart or grown in containers. Harvesting leaves from several plants, as opposed to all the leaves from one plant, will allow them to keep growing and extend your harvest. Hardly ever found for sale as a vegetable, land cress is almost like a gardener's secret – easy to grow and productive!

Spinach

This tasty, nutritious and easy-to-grow vegetable can be used as a salad leaf when young, or be allowed to grow fully and be harvested and cooked as a vegetable in its own right. If you are growing for cooking, you will need a lot of plants as the leaves wilt down to almost nothing, so if you have limited space, it may be best to grow for salads and buy frozen spinach for cooking. I do this as I would rather use the space for other crops, and because frozen spinach is quite cheap in the shops. By choosing the right variety for the time of year, you can grow spinach almost all year round, with early sowings from late winter (under cloches or fleece) continuing to late spring, followed by winter varieties sown in late summer. These later sowings can be covered again with cloches to extend the harvest, or grown in containers that can be placed in the greenhouse or cold frame over winter.

◄ Top: tree spinach; Centre: 'Amaze'; Bottom: 'Grewger' (Burger Leaf)

True spinach is not only fast growing, it can also be fast to bolt if you grow the wrong type for the time of year, or if the plants get too hot and stressed. It's best to read the packets before you buy the seeds, then you'll know you are selecting the right variety for what you want.

When sowing, the seed needs to be around 1cm (½in) deep in rows 30cm (12in) apart. As the plants grow you can harvest every other one to add to salads as young leaves, leaving the remainder to grow in the space you created. If you are only growing for smaller salad leaves, seeds can be scattered into a bed or pot, creating a cut-and-come-again crop for you to harvest as you like. You can start cutting around 2–3 weeks from germination and if you leave around 2–3cm (¾–1in) at the base of the plant, it will produce new, fresh leaves.

A great variety for smaller, sweeter leaves that can be left to grow bigger is 'Gigante d'Inverno'; as the name suggests, the leaves can become quite large, so it's a good multi-use variety as you won't need as many plants for a decent harvest. 'Rubino' is perfect to add colour to salads as it has a red midrib to the leaf; it's also fast growing and good in stir-fries.

There are other spinaches available that aren't technically real spinach; however, they are used in the same way and taste similar.

Tree spinach (aka Glitter spinach) is a spinach substitute that can grow up to 2m (6½ft) tall, producing an abundance of green leaves with a pink, glitter-like colouration to the underside. Smaller leaves can be used in salads, and they really do look pretty. However, larger leaves will need to be cooked.

New Zealand spinach is a creeping plant which has leaves that are thicker than regular spinach, almost succulent-like, so this means you don't need to harvest as many when wilting them down to eat. Often grown as an annual, this plant is a perennial and good to grow as a ground-cover vegetable.

Perpetual spinach is really a type of chard that tastes like, and can be used as, a spinach substitute. This plant performs well on dry soils where true spinach would run to seed, and it also grows well throughout autumn and winter without protection, making it a great alternative to grow on allotments, where watering can sometimes be a challenge.

Top Tips

- Keep lettuce plants well watered to prevent them from bolting and to prevent attacks from root aphid, which can affect lettuce grown in dry conditions.

- Growing your lettuce in the shadow of taller plants, such as runner beans, will help extend their life and prevent them bolting. This is because they thrive on dappled light rather than the full glare of the sun.

- Growing in the cooler months of spring and autumn will produce plants that will flower slower than those grown in the height of summer. Growing in fertile, moist soil will encourage plants to produce more tender growth than those grown in dry conditions.

- All salad leaves can be kept in the fridge for 7–10 days in a sealed bag with a piece of damp kitchen paper, which prevents the leaves from drying out and wilting.

- Land cress may not be perennial, but if you allow one or two to flower and set seed, you will have a constant supply. Just pull up any unwanted plants and add them to your salads or soups.

- The leaves of true spinach can taste bitter sometimes, which is due to the soil not being rich enough. Adding organic matter, such as homemade compost, will prevent this. Growing plants in semi-shade and keeping them well watered will also prolong their harvesting window.

Chard

Sometimes known as Swiss chard (because it was named by a Swiss botanist) or leaf beet, as these plants are related to beetroot but don't form a root, chard is grown for its leaves and stems, which come in a range of colours from yellow to white, red and pink. Pretty enough to add to an ornamental border, while looking fantastic in the vegetable garden, chard is a nutritious, easy-to-grow alternative to spinach and the leaves can be used like spring greens, while the midribs can be braised, stir-fried or added to soups. Chard will happily grow through the colder months and can be cropped all winter; come spring the plants will start to produce more fresh leaves and flower spikes, which can be cooked and eaten in soups and casseroles. If you leave a plant to flower, it will become a statuesque beacon of colour in the garden, plus you'll be able to harvest your own seeds from the plant! Whether you want leaves for salads, stir-fries, soups or casseroles, chard is the plant you need in the garden, if not for its productiveness then for its looks.

How to grow

Seed can be sown directly into the ground or started in modules around 1–2cm (½–¾in) deep. They only take a week or two to germinate and the roots of the plant are the same colour as the stems, making for stunning seedlings if you transplant module-grown plants. Plants can be grown in rows 30cm (12in) apart or dotted around the garden or flower border, happily growing in any fertile, well-drained soil. Chard likes rich soil but prefers it to have been manured or have had compost added the autumn before planting to ensure good leaf production for months on end.

Chard to grow

'Bright Lights' – Perhaps the most well-known and handsome of the chard varieties. This mix of different-coloured plants not only creates a fantastic display in the garden, it also looks great in a salad when young or on your plate when steamed or sautéed like spinach. Producing red, orange and yellow-stemmed plants, 'Bright Lights' is one of the most colourful vegetables you can grow.

'Peppermint' – Another coloured variety, this time in two-tone pink and white, as the name suggests. However, that's where the similarity to its name ends, as this plant doesn't taste like peppermint, but has the traditional, earthy chard taste. The slightly Savoy cabbage-like leaves of this plant work well in vegetable soups, where they add texture and colour. It looks stunning in the garden, too.

'Lucullus' – A larger chard. It's productive, with wide leaves, and is named after the Roman general of the same name, presumably because he was renowned for his lavish parties with lots of food, and this chard produces a lot! It may not be the most exciting colour, but this lime-green-leaved, white-stemmed variety is the most productive by far.

'Rhubarb' – A bright-red-stemmed, dark-green-leaved variety that really does look like its namesake. There are plenty of stories of new gardeners getting muddled up and making a rhubarb crumble with this variety; however, I'm not sure it would go that well with custard! When growing 'Rhubarb' make sure to label it well and don't harvest in a hurry.

Top Tips

- Don't compost the plant in spring, but wait for it to produce a new flush of tender, young leaves before it flowers.

- You can easily save your own seeds, just wait for the plant to start getting taller as it produces its flower spikes. Once seeds are formed, harvest the stalk and let it dry completely before rubbing the seeds from the stalk and storing in paper bags.

◄ 'Peppermint'
▼ Bolting chard

Mustard Leaves

Forget the spicy, yellow condiment that is served with beef, these leaves are totally different. Mustard leaves can be grown for use as a salad leaf or for cooking as they become more mature. Eaten raw, the leaves have a pleasant heat that's a little like rocket, while they become a lot milder when cooked. I like to add finely chopped leaves to soups and casseroles; you don't really notice them, but you still get one of your five a day. Hardly ever found for sale, you may come across a leaf or two in a mixed salad bag, but that's about it. Plants do tend to bolt quickly, so they should only really be grown in the cooler months of the year, avoiding mid-summer. Far from being a negative, this means you'll have a delicious, easy-to-grow, weather-hardy vegetable that you can grow in a greenhouse or outside in the winter months.

How to grow

Seeds can be sown outside in rows or scattered where they are to grow if you want a mustard leaf patch. Simply sprinkle the seed and ruffle the soil with your fingers to work them in, then water and wait for germination. Within a couple of weeks you'll have seedlings that can be used as a baby leaf in salads and sandwiches, while others are left to grow and keep you in fresh leaves for cooking. If you want to grow leaves over winter, start them off in early autumn, either in the garden direct or in modules, in an unheated greenhouse, before planting them out when large enough to handle. Protecting the young plants with a cloche will extend the harvest period. Alternatively, grow a few in the greenhouse in winter, as it's a great way to use the space.

Mustard leaves to grow

'Wasabino' – A pretty, serrated leaf variety which (as the name suggests) is quite spicy, tasting somewhat like wasabi. Great to add interest to salads, the leaves are best used young and smooth, as they become a little hairier as the plants mature. Sow seeds every couple of weeks to keep you in young leaves.

'Red Giant' – The red-flushed green leaves can become quite large as the plant grows. Excellent in salads, where it adds a pleasant taste that isn't too hot, while larger leaves are ideal to stir-fry or sauté with a little garlic. This variety copes well with winter weather and is very productive.

'Green in Snow' – This is, as the name implies, a very hardy variety that will happily shrug off a snow shower without any protection at all, so it's perfect for both the allotment and containers near the back door, where it can be harvested with ease.

◀ Harvesting mixed mustard leaves from the greenhouse

Top Tips

- After you have removed tomatoes from your greenhouse in autumn, sow the mustard-leaf seeds in the same beds or containers – there's no need to remove the tomato roots, just cut the old plants off at soil level and sprinkle in the seeds. The plants will grow all winter, giving you spicy leaves to enjoy right through to early spring, when they begin to flower. The small yellow flowers make a spicy addition to salads.

- Put harvested leaves in a zip lock bag with a piece of damp kitchen paper, which will help keep them fresh for 5–7 days.

Pak Choi

Pak choi can be used in stir-fries and soups, salads and pickles and is perhaps best-known for being a staple dish in Chinese restaurants throughout the country. Typically sold as green-leaved varieties with a white leaf stalk, this crunchy, somewhat mild-flavoured vegetable also comes in green leaf stalk and red-leaved varieties to grow at home. Quick-growing, pak choi can be used to 'intercrop' between cabbages, cauliflowers and even leeks, meaning they will be harvested before the slower-growing veg overshadow the speedy bulbous-bottomed pak choi. This also has the benefit of providing a little shade for the pak choi, as they can bolt (run to seed) quickly if grown in too much sun and heat. That said, the flowering stalk, along with the rest of the whole plant (above ground) is edible. The leaf stalks are crisp and juicy, while the leaves wilt quickly when cooked, giving two different textures in one mouthful. Young seedlings under 10cm (4in) tall are known as 'chicken feather' stage in China and are used whole in salads, whereas anything larger is best cooked to make the leaf stalk more palatable.

How to grow

Seeds only need to be sown 1cm (½in) deep and are best sown directly as they don't always perform as well if transplanted, they can bolt quicker in drier growing conditions. When sowing, you can broadcast the seeds if you want to grow them for smaller 'chicken feathers', or sow them in rows for mature plants, with a final spacing of 15–20cm (6–8in) depending on the variety.

Harvesting and storing

You can harvest single leaves from larger varieties, allowing them to grow on; alternatively, smaller pak choi can be harvested whole. To store, place in the fridge within a plastic bag or wrap in paper towel to maintain dryness and prevent the leaves from wilting. They can be refrigerated for around a week. It's best to handle this leafy green with care, as its leaves are delicate and susceptible to bruising.

Pak choi to grow

'Rubi' and 'Purple Rain' – Both produce deep purple leaves on pale green leaf stalks, perfect to add interest to your dish no matter what stage you harvest them at. Fast growing, they can be harvested at baby leaf stage only 30 days after sowing.

'Macau' – This looks more like a traditionally coloured pak choi, and if you want baby plants to add whole to soups and stir-fries, this is the one for you. Best grown in a grid pattern at 5cm (2in) spacings, this variety will be ready to harvest around 45–50 days from sowing – the perfect mini pak choi.

Top Tips

- Sow a row or two every couple of weeks to keep you in fresh plants

- Traditionally the leaves are dried and added to soups in the winter months, so if you have an excess or don't eat all your plants, try drying or dehydrating them for use later in the year.

◀ 'Macau'
▼ Pak choi intercropped with leeks

Sea Kale (Perennial)

This Victorian favourite is seldom seen in the shops and hardly ever spotted in gardens any more, yet it's a great perennial vegetable. Preferring to grow in the garden as opposed to containers, due to its long tap root, plants will grow well in the open border or in raised beds as long as the soil is well drained. Sea kale produces waxy, grey-green leaves that have a cabbage look about them, and are usually forced in late winter by placing a forcer or bucket over the plant to exclude light. You'll be rewarded with pale green shoots which have a flavour akin to asparagus and celery, with a little nutty bitterness to them. Sea kale does seem to be making a comeback in many seasonal restaurants where chefs want to cook with what's in season each month, yet it's almost impossible to buy in the shops, so it's the perfect veg to grow yourself.

How to grow

You can start plants from seed, but they are like rock-hard little bullets and need softening in warm water before you sow them in sandy, free-draining compost in spring or autumn. It's far more reliable, and easier, to grow plants from a root cutting, also known as a thong. You can buy thongs or plants online, and they are best potted up in winter, ready to plant out in spring. Lay out thongs in a tray filled with 5–10cm (2–4in) of sandy compost, then cover with a further 2–3cm (¾–1¼in) and keep them on a warm windowsill until they begin to grow. Plants should be transplanted in late spring after the frosts to where they are to grow, planting out with 60cm (24in) between plants if you are growing more than one.

Harvesting and storing

The first shoots and leaves can be harvested with a sharp knife in early spring. Traditionally the forced stems are steamed and served with hollandaise sauce, while the larger leaves are cooked like regular kale, yet they have a more minerally, seaweedy flavour to them. Older leaves can be tough and don't make for great eating, making this a truly seasonal vegetable.

Top Tips

- Don't try to force your plants until they are at least two years old, as this process takes a lot of the plant's energy, and they need to be established to survive forcing.

- Once established, take root cuttings after four or five years to replace the previous plants as they start to lose vigour and their health deteriorates.

- Plants produce large clusters of white flowers that have a sweet fragrance and taste like honey. No wonder they are adored by pollinators, but also by gardeners for adding to salads.

▼ Sea kale flowers

Celery

This can be a controversial vegetable, with very strong opinions on either side of the love it/hate it argument. Traditionally this was a more complicated, fussy vegetable to grow, and it wasn't the quickest to crop either, because you had to trench the plants. Trenching celery needs earth mounded up around the stems to make them pale and tender, which used to be done by growing them in actual trenches and filling it back in with soil as the plants grew, creating the blanched stems that were required. You could also wrap cardboard around the base of the plants to keep the sunlight out, creating the same effect, but it's still not the simplest thing to do. Nowadays, modern breeding has thankfully resulted in self-blanching varieties that are tender without the need for all the extra work – you simply grow them in blocks close together, rather than in rows.

No matter which types you grow, all celery like a fertile, moist site, as its wild ancestor grows in marshy ground and boggy riverbanks; so, make sure to add manure to the bed in the autumn before planting and keep well watered. I'm going to concentrate on the self-blanching types as they are easier to grow and more popular than the trenching ones.

Celery is a thirsty crop and drying out can cause plants to become stringy and bolt, which is not what you want if tender stems for salads is your goal. Celery can be harvested when it gets to the size you like, but remember that a hard frost will kill the plants, so they need picking before then. As a bonus crop, you can use the leaves of stem celery to help flavour stocks and soups, so don't consign them to the compost heap straightaway!

How to grow

Seeds can be started directly in the garden, but I find that slugs seem to decimate the seedlings before they can grow and therefore I start mine in small modules. Celery can prematurely bolt later in its life if it's sown in too cold a temperature, so make sure it doesn't drop below 10°C (50°F) for more than 10–12 hours (overnight usually). Once seedlings are large enough to handle, harden them off well before you plant them out, as otherwise they can suffer from transplant shock, which makes them bolt early. Try not to disturb the roots as you plant them into their final growing place. Self-blanching varieties can be planted out at ground level at around 20–22cm (8–9in) apart in a block. This allows them to shade each other and it helps aid blanching. Then the most important thing is water, and lots of it!

Celery to grow

'Blush' – A gorgeous rose-bottomed celery that graduates to light green towards the top of the plant. It's a self-blanching variety, so there's no messing around with earthing up, leaving you to enjoy the crunchy stems as you like.

'Golden Self-blanching' – One of the first self-blanching types, originating in the 1880s. This paler, creamy-green stalked variety is still around because of its superior flavour compared to many shop-bought varieties, plus it's almost totally stringless at the heart.

'Par-Cel' – An unusual celery that's worth including in your veg plot because it's perhaps the easiest variety to grow! I must admit, it doesn't produce crunchy stems, as it's actually grown for the leaves. Looking like parsley but tasting like celery (hence the name), and producing finely cut leaves on a compact plant, it's used more like a herb than a vegetable. Great with fish, used in soups and stocks, or tossed through salads.

- To get the most from your plants always keep them moist. In the summer, when the plants have become established, feed them once with a high-nitrogen fertiliser such as chicken manure.

◄ Celery seedlings

Celeriac

Celery's little known relative. Also known as 'root celery' because of its larger, more bulbous shape, it is in fact a swollen stem, not a root at all. Celeriac is far superior to celery in my eyes, being a much more refined and useful vegetable in the kitchen, and easier to grow. With its meatier texture and more delicate taste, it's the perfect vegetable to make into soups, add to winter casseroles or grate raw into salads; they are even delicious cut into steaks and braised in butter.

How to grow

Similar to celery, celeriac is best sown in modules or trays and pricked out when large enough to handle. These fragrant little plants not only look the same as celery at this stage, but they also have the same fresh, almost herby fragrance. Once the last frosts have passed, transplant the seedlings around 30cm (12in) apart and keep them well watered as they thrive on moisture. As the root begins to swell, you may find that the lower leaves droop to the soil and need removing, which can be done by gently pulling it from the plant, creating the distinct shape and scars of a celeriac.

Harvesting and storing

It's best to harvest your celeriac before the first frost, by lifting the root from the ground with a fork/spade, then removing the roots and shaking the plant to remove most of the soil. You can use the leaves in stocks and soups as you would celery if you wish, as they add a great flavour. The clean, leaf-free roots can be stored easily by placing them in boxes of damp compost or sand in a cold (but frost-free) environment – a garage or shed will be fine. If this seems like too much work, you can also leave your celeriac outside in the ground, covering them with a thick layer of leaves and pegging horticultural fleece over the top to keep them in. This keeps the edible part of the plant in good condition, as long as you check them for pest damage periodically.

Celeriac to grow

'Brilliant' is a smooth, almost white-skinned variety that has a deliciously delicate flavour, and the flesh does not discolour as fast as some older varieties.

'Mars' is a modern celeriac which has been bred to stay in the ground longer, easily lasting until mid-winter. It has more upright leaves, which means they suffer from less mud splatter in rainy weather.

Top Tips

- Choose a modern variety to grow, as these will have far smoother skin and be less likely to bolt.

- Just like celery, celeriac likes lots of water. As a gardening friend once said to me, 'when you walk past it, water it!' And, this is advise I have listened to ever since.

◄ 'Mars'
▼ Keeping plants well watered

Florence Fennel

Unlike herb fennel, which is grown for its flavoursome fronds, Florence fennel is prized for its swollen leaf stem, which some refer to as a 'bulb'. This anise-flavoured Mediterranean classic is a true gourmet vegetable and a sun worshipper, so don't be tempted to sow seeds too early or leave plants in the garden too late, as the frosts will kill them off. Being the Goldilocks of the vegetable world, needing the conditions to be 'just right', plants benefit from a site that's had compost or manure worked into it the autumn before, and constant moisture. It may sound like a fussy veg, but fennel is well worth growing, in my eyes. I love it in salads or sliced in half and braised on the barbecue, and I couldn't do without a fennel and potato gratin. Fennel can be quite pricey in the shops, so growing a few at home is worth the effort, plus the fronds can be used as herb fennel in salads, making it a two-for-one crop!

How to grow

Plants don't like root disturbance, and this can cause premature bolting, so if starting seeds indoors I always use small modules and sow the seeds singly so there is no damage caused by removing a weaker plant. You can also start seed directly outside in mid-summer; just make sure, when thinning plants, to cut them off at ground level instead of pulling them up, as again, this reduces root disturbance to the remaining plants. Thinnings can be added to salads. When your plants are growing, keep them moist – by mulching around the plants with compost to prevent water evaporation – and it's also beneficial to feed plants every two weeks with a high-potash feed to encourage bigger 'bulbs'.

Harvesting and storing

Start by removing the delicate fronds and stems from the bulbs, storing them separately in a plastic bag or container to keep them crisp. It's best not to wash the bulbs until you're ready to use them, as moisture can lead to premature spoilage. When stored properly in the fridge, Florence fennel can remain fresh for 3–5 days, but to extend its shelf life further, consider wrapping in damp kitchen paper before placing inside a sealed plastic bag – by doing this, your fennel should stay fresh for 10-14 days.

Florence fennel to grow

'Dragon' F1 – A great variety to grow at home as it produces large bulbs with a rounder shape and good bolting resistance, meaning it's not as temperamental as some of the others available.

'Zefa Fino' – This variety has gained an AGM (Award of Garden Merit) from the RHS (Royal Horticultural Society) and produces flatter-shaped bulbs that are a little taller than 'Dragon', and they also have a slightly greener colour to them, rather than bright white.

- Thinly sliced fennel and onion can be tossed in a little olive oil and apple cider vinegar for a light salad dish to go with barbecued meats and fish.

- The fennel fronds can also be chopped and added to ice cube trays with some white wine, and frozen, which is useful for adding to sauces or fish dishes later in the year.

◄ Top: 'Zefa Fino';
Bottom: 'Dragon' F1

Sweetcorn

This must be one of the most highly anticipated crops in my garden, simply because of the taste of the home-grown cobs! If you have never grown your own sweetcorn, you are missing a treat, as the ones you buy are nothing, and I mean NOTHING, like the ones you can grow yourself. You simply can't beat the sweetness in flavour and tenderness of a freshly harvested cob that you've just cooked. In fact, some of mine don't reach the kitchen because they are so juicy and sweet you can eat them fresh from the plant.

Forget the fields of towering plants you see on the TV, there are shorter varieties that can be grown in raised beds and even large containers. I grow my sweetcorn in half of a raised bed measuring only 1.2m (4ft) square, with 16 plants that produce around 22–25 cobs each year, so don't think you need acres to grow them in. I even grow other crops in the same bed, including dwarf French beans around the edge and a pumpkin that I train around the bed in the middle; that's three crops from the one bed. Unlike most vegetables, sweetcorn is wind-pollinated, meaning the pollen from one plant needs to blow onto the next to pollinate it – no insects are involved. For this reason, your plants need to be grown in a block or square formation, ideally as wide as they are long, so 4 x 4, 5 x 5. It's a good idea to shake the plants every day once you see the tell-tale tassels appear, as this action results in better cob formation. If you've ever had cobs that weren't full with kernels missing, this is because of poor pollination.

How to grow

I find it best to sow the seed in root trainers or deep modules, as the roots on sweetcorn appreciate more space than most other veg. Sow around 3cm (1¼in) deep and don't let the compost dry out. As they like hot summers, it's worth growing varieties that are bred to grow well in the UK, and give them the sunniest space you can. Once seedlings are around 15–20cm (6–8in) tall you can plant them out into the garden as long as all chance of frost has passed. If you have the space, you can plant them 35–45cm (14–18in) apart in a grid, but I plant mine 30cm (12in) apart and still get a great crop each year. Adding plenty of compost or manure to the bed before you transplant your seedlings will help get the most from your plants, and you can earth them up a little with soil as they are growing if you see the roots above soil level, which also stops them rocking in the wind.

Harvesting and storing

When it comes to testing if your cobs are ripe and ready to harvest, make sure the tassels that protrude from the end of the cobs are dry and brown, then carefully peel back a leaf from the cob and push your fingernail into a kernel to release the juice. If this juice is clear the cob needs longer on the plant; if it's milky it is ready to harvest. To remove the cob, hold and twist it while also holding the plant; this will prevent you from snapping the stalk. Sweetcorn cobs lose their sweetness quickly, so it's best to pick them when you need them; however, too long on the plant will result in a starchy-tasting cob, so this really is a gourmet, seasonal crop to grow.

Sweetcorn to grow

When it comes to classifying sweetcorn, there are different types, from standard (su) old-fashioned sweetcorn, sugar-enhanced (se) to supersweet (sh2), synergistic (sy) and augmented supersweet. It all sounds quite complicated, but they are all grown in the same way, with most seed companies simply calling them standard or supersweet.

Standard (su) sweetcorn, such as 'Sundance' and 'Golden Bantam', are great tasting, but their sweetness turns into starch very quickly. If you leave them in the fridge until the next day they are half as sweet as when first picked, and the kernels are also quite tough and can be chewy. Plants should not be grown near other corn as they can become starchy if they cross-pollinate. If you want to grow something a little different-looking, try 'Blue Jade', which produces shorter 90cm (3ft) plants that are good for exposed plots, with small, steel-blue cobs that have little sweetness but instead taste more like corn-flavoured mashed potatoes, making them great for barbecuing.

Sugar-enhanced (se) varieties will retain their sweetness for 2–4 days in the fridge and have a softer kernel, making them easier to chew, as well as juicier.

Supersweet (sh2) types have up to twice the amount of sugar as standard types and are a little more tender. 'Moonshine' and 'Goldcrest' have a deliciously sweet taste and can be stored for up to 7–10 days without losing too much sweetness. They need higher temperatures to germinate and shouldn't be grown together or they can cross-pollinate and produce different-coloured kernels on the cobs or become starchy.

Synergistic (sy) types, such as 'Illusion' and 'Inferno', have an even sweeter taste and tender kernels that are easier to chew and make them ideal for eating fresh from the plant without the need for cooking. These types don't need isolating from su and sh2 varieties, but, they can't cope with cold soil so are best started in modules and transplanted or sown later. 'Picasso' F1 is a fantastic sweetcorn with white and yellow kernels and red-flushed leaves and stalks, plus bright pink tassels, making this variety really stand out in the garden. The cobs are incredibly sweet and juicy, and as they are around 20cm (8in) long they fit easily in a pan for cooking.

Augmented supersweet are the very latest breeding, combining the sweetness of sh2 with the softer texture and juiciness of se varieties, producing the perfect sweetcorn to eat raw. In fact, the cobs can be

eaten fresh from the plant as you would a piece of fruit, or stored in the fridge for over a week without losing sweetness. 'Pot of Gold' is an amazingly tasty dwarf variety that only gets to 1.5m (5ft) tall and can be grown in large containers, plus the shorter habit means it's a great one to grow on a windier site. The cobs are fatter and shorter than regular ones, which makes them perfect to fit in a pan if you manage to get out of the garden with them! 'Eden' F1 is a creamy-white cob variety, with very sweet, juicy kernels that are crisp with a tender skin.

Problems

Lodging is the bending or breaking of stems near the ground, causing the plants to lean or lie flat on the soil. This phenomenon is usually caused by factors such as strong winds, heavy rain or excessive application of nitrogen fertiliser, which can lead to rapid growth and weak stalks. You can counter this by earthing up your corn around the base, helping to hold the plants in place if strong winds are forecast. There are also varieties available that are less susceptible.

◄ Far left top: 'Jade Blue'; Far left bottom: 'Illusion'; Left: dwarf beans growing around the edge of the sweetcorn bed

rhubarb (Perennial)

This may be used as a fruit in most homes, yet it's technically a vegetable! That aside, rhubarb is a fantastic plant to grow as it's perennial and will crop for years with very little effort. It's also becoming more difficult to buy and is expensive when you do find it. I love rhubarb for its sweet tartness, especially in crumble but also as a compote to go with ice cream, or even yoghurt in the morning. As your plant will be in the same spot for a long time, it's best to make sure it's somewhere that's free of perennial weeds like nettles or dock and has lots of manure or compost worked into the site. Plants can be bought already growing in pots and planted out almost any time of year, but they are more economical to buy as root pieces known as crowns, which are best planted in autumn or spring before the root starts to grow.

How to grow

Growing your plants in full sun will produce the best crop, but they will grow in semi-shade as well, they just won't crop as much. When planting the crowns make sure it's a free-draining spot as standing water can cause your plant to rot during the winter. The top of the root should be around 3cm (1¼in) below soil level, but if your site is quite heavy with lots of clay, it's best to plant at soil level. As they establish, your plants will get quite large, needing around 80–100cm (2½–3ft) between plants to accommodate their large leaves. However, don't harvest from them in the first year as you want the plant to establish well before you start pulling. The leaves contain high amounts of oxalic acid and are therefore classed as poisonous to humans, so only eat the stalks, and always make sure small children are supervised around the plants. You would need to eat a lot of the leaf for it to be harmful, but nobody wants a bad tummy. After around five years, your plant may begin to lose its vigour and need splitting. This simply means you need to dig up the plant and chop it into sections (ideally 4–5), each with a growing tip, then remove any softer or rotting parts and replant the sections or give them away. Dividing is best done in early winter, or any time between autumn and spring while the plant is dormant.

Harvesting and storing

When harvesting stalks there is a trick to it – pull and twist, never cut. Cutting the stalk from the plant can cause it to rot back, whereas the easiest way to get the entire stalk is to hold it near the base and firmly pull while slightly twisting. By doing this the whole stalk should come off in your hand and you can then remove the leaf and the end that connected to the crown, leaving a lovely stalk of rhubarb.

If you want an even more gourmet treat from your plant you can force the stalks. This simply means you force the plant to grow early by covering it with a specialist forcer or old plastic bin so that no sunlight can get to it. By doing this in mid-winter you will be rewarded with pale-pink, sweeter-tasting stalks which are amazing in crumble, served with a little cream or ice cream. This process can take a lot of energy from your rhubarb, so it's best to only do this on established plants and remove the forcer in mid-spring, leaving the plant to recover, and then don't harvest from it for the rest of the year.

▶ Forcing rhubarb

Rhubarb to grow

'Victoria' – A traditional type which can only be harvested until early summer, then the oxalic acid builds up in the stalks and it can make them a little too sour (plus the plants need time to build up their energy to survive winter).

'Livingstone' – This is a modern, British-bred variety that crops all the way into autumn; this is because breeders have broken the summer dormancy period, meaning the plant just keeps growing. I have one of these in an open-bottomed raised bed and it crops very well indeed, plus the stalks are just about stringless, which can be an issue for older types.

'Poulton's Pride' – The very latest in rhubarb breeding, a rosy, red-stalked variety which is sweeter-tasting than most but still has enough 'tang' to please traditional rhubarb fans. Cropping for an incredible 10 months of the year from early spring to early winter, the once-short spring season of fresh rhubarb is now a thing of the past and you'll be eating it all year if you grow your own!

Problems

One common issue that us gardeners encounter is the untimely flowering of our rhubarb plants. When plants send up their flower stalks, it can divert valuable energy away from the development of the succulent stems. To combat this, it's essential to be vigilant and remove the entire flower stalk as soon as it appears, effectively redirecting the plant's energy towards producing more stalks. Simply cut the flower stalk off at ground level. It's worth noting that some rhubarb cultivars are more prone to flowering than others, and this phenomenon tends to occur more frequently after a wet summer or when an excessive amount of high-nitrogen fertiliser has been applied.

Top Tips

- Adding rhubarb leaves to the planting hole of cabbage family members is reputed to help stop club root, which is a disease that leads to swollen and distorted roots in root vegetables.

- When harvesting, only take up to a maximum of one-third of the stems at any one time, leaving the rest to keep growing. In spring, mulch around your plant with manure to help feed it and retain moisture as the summer warms up.

- Plants like to be kept well watered, otherwise they can begin to flower. If they do bloom, simply cut the flower off at the base and water well.

◄ Removing the rhubarb flower at the base

Asparagus (Perennial)

This must be one of the most cost-effective and rewarding perennial vegetables you can grow. Not only do home-grown spears taste far superior to even those sold in swanky farm shops, but you will have more than you know what to do with! Admittedly, the UK asparagus season is quite short, ranging from St George's Day to the Summer Solstice (23 April to 21 June), but I find that my plants start producing spears towards the end of March, which gives around 11–12 weeks of harvest. Not only will an established asparagus bed give you enough of a crop to make soup, quiches and steamed, boiled and baked asparagus, it will keep doing this for 20 years!

Home-grown asparagus come in the traditional green, which we are all used to, plus there are deep-purple-coloured varieties as well. In fact, you can even produce the tender white spears you find for sale on the continent; simply covering the spears with soil as they grow produces these ivory delights.

Older types of asparagus come in both female and male plants, with the latter producing thicker, bigger spears and the former, more slender ones, followed by red berries on the ferns. If you aren't too worried about this you can go ahead and grow any variety you want, but if you want the most from the space you are using it's best to opt for a more modern all-male variety, as you'll get a bigger harvest. You don't need both sexes to produce your asparagus as you eat the emerging stems of the plant before they begin to turn into a Christmas-tree-like fern, so all-male is the best choice – however, even these can sometimes produce a female plant. Lightly steaming asparagus is the traditional way to cook it, but I love the spears griddled in a cast-iron griddle pan with a little oil, then served with traditional hollandaise sauce or a squeeze of lemon juice, with butter melted on top. Other favourites include quiche, risotto and soup; or simply add them raw to salads for a flavour and texture sensation.

How to grow

Plants can be grown from seed if you want to start an asparagus bed cheaply, but it will take a couple of years for them to produce a good number of spears, and in my eyes it's a waste of a bed for that initial setup period. You are far better off starting plants from established crowns. You can buy these from the garden centre or from online suppliers; go for the largest available, it's worth the cost.

The key to growing asparagus successfully is a weed-free bed, so before planting make sure to remove all perennial and annual weeds and add them to the compost. The key time to plant asparagus crowns is when they are dormant, in late autumn or mid-spring time, as this allows them to settle in before they start to grow – they don't like to be disturbed. Add a bucket of well-rotted manure or compost per square metre of ground and fork it in, then dig a trench around 30cm (12in) wide and deep, adding 5cm (2in) of manure to the base, followed by 5cm (2in) of the excavated soil to form a ridge along the centre of the trench. Basically, you want to form a long mound down the centre so that when you place your crowns in the trench the growing tip points upwards and it sits on the mound, while the roots trail down the mound (think of how octopus tentacles look). Space your crowns out around 30cm (12in) apart to get the most from your bed, then carefully backfill the trench with a mix of

compost and the excavated soil, being careful not to damage the delicate roots. If you are growing more than one row of plants, you need around 45cm (18in) between the rows. Finally, water the area well and mulch with 5cm (2in) of well-rotted manure to help supress weeds and feed your new plants.

Harvesting and Storing

Now comes the hardest part of growing asparagus, as you need to leave them alone and not harvest them for two years, which lets them settle in and establish well. I know this seems like a long time, but I can't tell you how worthwhile it is to be patient, and how good your crop will finally taste. In year three you can harvest spears for around six weeks, letting the plants recover their strength for full-on harvesting the year after. To harvest, wait until the spears are around 20cm (8in) long, then cut them off about 2–3cm (¾–1¼in) below soil level with a sharp knife. You'll be surprised how quickly they grow, so check every two days and you'll likely have spears to harvest.

Problems

Keep an eye out for asparagus beetle, as these colourful little critters can decimate your plants. Adults can be picked off and disposed of, while the sticky eggs they lay can be spotted on the stems and wiped off with a piece of tissue paper.

Asparagus to grow

'Mondeo' – A disease-resistant green variety which is all-male and has impressive yields. In fact, the plants in my garden often produce spears thicker than my thumb, and they have a sweet, superior flavour. If you only want to grow a green variety, this is the one.

'Erasmus' – The world's first 100 per cent purple male asparagus, with others being male-dominant and still producing some female plants. Intensely purple in colour, this variety is early to crop and keeps its colour when cooked, plus it can be harvested lightly in year two, so you won't have to wait as long to try it.

'Vittorio' – One of the best plants if you want to produce tender, white spears. This is done by earthing up the emerging spears as they protrude from the plant, resulting in pale, extremely tender spears which are prized for their flavour. This variety will also produce green spears if left to grow as regular asparagus.

Top Tips

- Always harvest the spears, whether you need them or not, otherwise the plant will put energy into producing the fern and not into pushing up more spears.

- Always weed by hand as asparagus roots are very shallow and can be damaged by hoeing.

- To remove the tough base of a spear once harvested, never cut it with a knife, simply hold the spear at either end and slowly bend it; the spear will naturally snap to leave just the tender part.

- Spears will keep for longer if stored in a glass 5cm (2in) full of water in the fridge, pointed end upwards.

◄ 'Mondeo'
▼ Asparagus beetle

Globe Artichokes (Perennial)

These are one of the most statuesque plants you can grow in the veg garden – in fact, they are just at home at the back of the flower border, and that's where I grow mine! Producing large plants, globe artichokes are grown for their edible flower buds and shouldn't be confused with Jerusalem artichokes (see page 50), which are a root crop.

A favourite on the European continent, you'll find the large, thistle-like heads for sale in almost every market there, while restaurants offer them as a starter served with butter or vinaigrette, on top of pizzas, in salads or made into tasty dips. Home-grown plants will each produce around 10 buds per year, and if you don't harvest them, you will find that bees and butterflies adore the flowers as they open and reveal their fluffy, purple interior.

There are traditional green varieties and the more attractive purple ones, and both grow in the same way and look and taste almost the same when cooked, so it depends what colour you prefer when they are growing in the garden. Globe artichokes can be a little spiny on the leaves and flower buds, so make sure to plant them at the back of a border or away from a pathway.

How to grow

Plants can be started from seed pretty easily, or you can buy young plants to grow on. To start from seed, simply sow them into modules or small pots of peat-free compost around 1cm (½in) deep and keep them on a windowsill to germinate. You can sow the seeds from late winter to late spring, then make later sowings outside directly into the ground. Once seedlings are large enough to handle, they need potting on into a larger container before being hardened off for 10–14 days, then planted out around 80–90cm (32–36in) apart. Plants will reach between 1.2–1.5m (4–5ft) wide and tall, so make sure to give them plenty of space.

Harvesting and storing

Small buds can be harvested without the choke in late spring. Simply cut the bud from the plant, being careful of the sharp spikes on the tips of the leaves, then you can either leave the plants to grow on and flower or cut them down to ground level and they will produce a fresh flush of leaves and buds around 8 weeks later.

Globe artichokes to grow

'Violet de Provence' – A beautiful variety, with purple and green mottled buds. It's also reputed to be finer-tasting than most of the green varieties and looks spectacular in the garden. One of the first to crop, you should be harvesting your first buds in late spring.

'Gros Vert de Laon' – A green variety which is later-cropping, with the largest buds of any artichoke. Plants may need staking or supporting in windier areas, but it's well worth the effort to see these plants flower.

▼ 'Violet de Provence'

Top Tips

- After a couple of years your plants will produce offsets. These are small plants that are attached to the main plant and can be carefully removed, along with a few roots, and potted up to create new plants for free.

- During the autumn, it's a good idea to mulch around your plant with well-rotted manure or compost to provide a little protection to the roots for the winter.

Vegetable Fruits

While many vegetables take the spotlight for their edible leaves, shoots, stems or roots, there's an array of delectable options grown specifically for their fruits, which can often steal the show. These fruiting vegetables span a wide spectrum of flavours and textures. Some are grown for their crispness and refreshing qualities, while others tickle the tastebuds with a blend of sweetness and tanginess. And then there are those devilish varieties that pack a spicy punch – their fruit used more as a flavour enhancer rather than a standalone vegetable.

It's worth noting that the majority of fruiting vegetables originate from warmer corners of the world. Consequently, in the UK, many of these plants benefit greatly from the shelter of a greenhouse or tunnel to replicate those hotter growing conditions. However, thanks to advances in breeding, there are now varieties specially tailored to thrive in cooler and damper summers, even when grown outdoors.

Think of foreign holidays when you've enjoyed luscious tomatoes, crisp peppers, succulent aubergines, or piquant chillies while basking in the sun. Why not bring a taste of those much-loved flavours to your very own vegetable patch or garden?

When it comes to growing vegetables with exceptional flavours, chilli peppers and sweet peppers stand out as top choices for me. These vibrant and versatile plants offer a wide range of varieties that are rarely found in supermarkets. While many people associate chilli peppers with the familiar 'Jalapeno' shape, which transforms from green to red, or the fiery 'Scotch Bonnet' that can bring tears to your eyes, there are heat levels and colourful varieties to suit every palate.

Chilli peppers come in a plethora of colours, including yellow, orange, purple and even striped, making the options for home-growing truly diverse. To simplify matters, I'll refer to any variety with heat as a chilli pepper, while those without heat will be classified as sweet peppers.

To get the most out of your plants, these sun-lovers are ideally grown in greenhouses, polytunnels or protected environments. However, there are certain varieties that can thrive and produce crops in containers or hanging baskets, making them suitable for outdoor growing in sunny spaces. This means that regardless of your available growing area, there is a chilli or pepper variety to suit your needs – there are even chillies that are compact enough to grow in tin cans, and perennial ones that come back each year!

Sweet peppers display a vast range of shapes, including the large blocky ones commonly found in supermarkets, as well as long, pointed ones, snack-sized and even slender varieties that closely resemble chilli peppers. These sweeter-tasting peppers typically have thick and juicy flesh, making them suitable for both eating raw and cooking. However, there are also some sweet peppers with thinner flesh that are perfect for pickling, grilling or adding to pizzas. I'm going to focus on smaller-sized sweet pepper plants and those that thrive well in home gardens, excluding the commonly available, large, blocky ones.

The world of chilli peppers offers an astonishing array of shapes, sizes and heat levels that can truly be mind-boggling. Instead of mentioning the ordinary or widely known varieties, I want to provide a glimpse of lesser-known chilli pepper varieties that may surprise and intrigue you. Once you lay your eyes on these unique varieties, you'll likely be inspired to grow them yourself.

Chilli peppers are particularly appealing for their ability to provide an abundance of flavourful fruit while requiring minimal space – and if you choose the right variety, a single plant can easily produce enough fruit to satisfy the average family's needs.

The Scoville Heat Unit rating (SHU), named after American pharmacist Wilbur Scoville, is a measurement scale used to quantify the heat or spiciness of chilli peppers. The scale is based on the concentration of capsaicin, the compound responsible for the pungent sensation in chilli peppers – the higher the number, the hotter the chilli.

Chilies & Peppers

How to grow

When it comes to growing chilli peppers and sweet peppers, there are some general guidelines regarding their growth and how long they take to crop. Typically, the hotter the chilli pepper, the longer it takes to grow and produce fruit. Similarly, larger-fruited sweet peppers tend to require a longer growing period. However, it's important to note that there can always be exceptions to these rules, so it's advisable to refer to the information provided on the seed packet for specific sowing and cropping times.

For both types of peppers, you can start sowing seeds from mid-winter if you have access to grow lights and a heated propagator to create an environment that protects them until the last frosts have passed. However, if you are starting them on a windowsill without additional heating, it is better to wait until late winter or early spring before sowing. This delay ensures that the seedlings don't become leggy or stretched due to insufficient light early in the year.

When starting, I use peat-free compost and sow seeds around 1cm (½in) deep in individual modules. These modules are then placed in a heated propagator set at around 20°C (68°F). Alternatively, you can start them on a sunny windowsill and cover the containers with a plastic bag to retain moisture. It usually takes about 2–3 weeks for the seeds to germinate. Once germination occurs, remove the plastic bag or propagator lid to allow for air circulation. Continue growing the seedlings at around 16°C (60°F) until they are large enough to handle. At this point, transplant them into 9–10cm (3½–4in) pots, ensuring they remain warm and adequately watered. As roots start appearing through the bottom of each container, it's time to pot them on into larger ones. Once your plants reach a height of 15cm (6in), it is recommended to pinch out the growing tip. This simple act encourages the plants to become bushier, resulting in more flowers and fruit being produced; without this intervention, the plants tend to grow tall and leggy. However, it's important to consider the final height of your chosen variety – if a plant naturally stays under 30cm (12in) tall and is already bushy, there is no need to pinch out the growing tip.

The timing for transplanting your peppers depends on where you want to grow them. If you have a heated greenhouse, you can transfer them to their final growing place in mid-spring. For an unheated greenhouse or polytunnel, late spring is the ideal time for planting them out. As for outdoor varieties and those intended for hanging baskets, early summer is the best month for planting. When selecting containers, a width and depth of 30cm (12in) is generally recommended for most larger pepper varieties, while smaller ones can be grown in pots with a diameter of 15cm (6in) or more – and hanging baskets and troughs work well too. If planting in the ground, ensure a spacing of 40–45cm (16–18in) between plants and 30cm (12in) for dwarf varieties. If you're growing in the ground, it's beneficial to incorporate well-rotted manure into the soil before planting, as this will ensure a bountiful harvest, with approximately three spades of well-rotted manure per square metre being a suitable amount to add.

For taller pepper varieties, it may be necessary to provide support using canes or string suspended from the roof of your greenhouse or tunnel. This system helps to bear the weight of ripening fruit and prevents the plants collapsing under their own weight.

Most chillies and peppers are treated as annual plants, with new seeds sown each year, but certain chilli pepper varieties, such as Rocoto chillies, can be overwintered in a frost-free location. By doing so, they can regrow the following year and start producing crops earlier. At the end of the growing season, simply prune the plant back to a 15cm (6in) stem from the base and trim any branches on the remaining stem to 5cm (2in) in length. Personally, I keep my plants in a lean-to that maintains a temperature of 6–8°C (43–46°F) during the winter, as this cool environment prevents the plant producing new growth. Then, when spring arrives and the light intensity increases, I gradually raise the temperature to provide more warmth. This stimulates the plant to come back to life, triggering new growth and earlier flowering compared to plants grown from seed.

By overwintering specific chilli pepper varieties, you can benefit from a head start in the growing season and enjoy an earlier harvest. It's important to note that not all chilli pepper varieties can be successfully overwintered, so it's advisable to research the specific requirements of your chosen variety and provide suitable conditions for its successful regrowth. That said, it's worth trying it with your favourite plants, as they will only be composted otherwise.

▶ 'Scallywag'

Harvesting and storing

Chillies and peppers offer incredible versatility, as they can be harvested and consumed at various stages of growth – from immature to fully ripe, with everything in between.

When peppers are harvested in their immature stage, they tend to have a savoury flavour. On the other hand, chillies are less spicy when they first develop and gradually increase in heat as they ripen to their final colour. Sweet peppers, in general, become sweeter as they ripen, and they also change colour.

To harvest the fruit, it is best to cut them from the plant instead of pulling them off, as pulling can cause damage. Once harvested, the fruit can be stored in the refrigerator for a couple of weeks, and can be used raw or cooked, pickled, dried or even ground into powder.

For sweet peppers, remove the core and seeds and freeze the flesh in freezer bags for later use in casseroles, soups and sauces; this works well for dishes where the flesh needs to be soft and tender, rather than crisp. As for milder chillies, slicing and pickling them is a great way to preserve them, plus they make an excellent addition to burgers. To pickle them, first sterilise your jars; wash them in hot soapy water and then place them in a hot oven at 180°C (350°F) for 15 minutes. Meanwhile, slice the chillies and prepare a pickling brine by combining 250ml (1 cup) vinegar, 250ml (1 cup) water, 1 tablespoon of salt and a few spices – such as black peppercorns and coriander seeds – and heat until the salt dissolves. Pop the sliced chillies into the sterilised jars and pour over the hot brine, ensuring they are fully submerged. Seal the jars and store in a cool, dark place for several months.

Another preservation option is drying. Simply string the chillies or peppers together using a needle and thread, creating a garland. Hang the garland in a warm, well-ventilated area away from direct sunlight. Alternatively, you can use a food dehydrator or an oven set to a low temperature (around 50°C/122°F – you may need to prop the door open if your oven doesn't go that low) to dry the peppers until crisp. This can take anything from 4–12 hours depending on the thickness of the flesh. Once the peppers are completely dried and brittle, store them in airtight containers in a cool, dry place. Dried peppers and chillies can last for a year or more.

Perhaps the easiest storage method for chillies is freezing. Simply wash and dry them, pop them into freezer bags, then freeze them whole. This way, you can remove as many as needed whenever you want to add a little or a lot of heat to your cooking. There's no need to defrost them, just slice the frozen chilli or add it whole.

Chillies and peppers to grow

Peppers

'Nardello' – This renowned pepper is highly sought-after for frying and remains a popular choice among growers today. Originally grown by the Nardello family, who have preserved this true Italian heirloom since the 19th century, it boasts a productive harvest throughout the summer season. The elongated fruits have a tapered shape, typically measuring around 20–25cm (8–10in), and grow on plants that reach a height of 60–90cm (2–3ft). Notably, this pepper has recently gained recognition for being the sweetest non-bell-shaped pepper available when fully ripe. Due to its great qualities, 'Nardello' excels in roasted and fried dishes, brings exceptional flavour to pasta sauces, and adds a refreshing crunch to salads.

'Popti' F1 – If you like sweet peppers but often end up with half left in the fridge, 'Popti' is the pepper you need to grow, producing smaller fruit that are 6–8cm (2½–3in) long and 5cm (2in) wide – the perfect size for using the full fruit in one go. Not only that, but this compact variety also only grows to 45cm (18in) tall, so it is ideal for growing in the smallest of greenhouses or in a container outside. Expect around 10 fruits from each of these petite plants – the ideal option for those with limited space.

'Redskin' F1 – A compact plant that will thrive in a large hanging basket, making growing peppers even easier! This award-winning variety is perfect for those with no greenhouse and only limited space, but it's also a great plant to grow in containers.

'Peppers From Heaven Orange' F1 – Produces lots of slightly elongated, orange, sweet peppers from compact plants. The crisp-fleshed fruit are perfect to use like any other pepper, but plants can be grown in the smallest of spaces, or even hanging baskets, bringing a burst of bright orange to your garden.

'Aji Cachucha Purple Splotched' – Also known as the Puerto Rican pepper, because that is where it was first discovered, this Caribbean variety is recognised for its mild and sweet taste. It belongs to the Aji Cachucha group of peppers and is primarily used as a cooking or seasoning pepper, as it has a beautiful

Top Tips

- Keep greenhouses and polytunnels below 30°C (86°F) in summer, as higher temperatures can reduce the number of fruit that the plants produce. Consider using shading, keeping the doors and windows open, and damping down once or twice a day to increase humidity, as peppers will appreciate this.

- Wear gloves when handling hot chilli seeds and fruit, as they can cause irritation if you rub your eyes (or any other delicate area).

- Like tomatoes, peppers can suffer from blossom end rot, so make sure your watering is consistent and regular. Consider adding a mulch to the soil surface to retain more moisture.

◄ Top left: 'Scallywag'; Top right: 'Nardello'; Centre left: 'Buena Mulata' Centre right: 'Peppers From heaven Yellow' F1; Bottom left: 'Peppapeach' Bottom right: 'Peppers from Heaven Orange' F1

▼ Damping down the greenhouse floor

flavour. Starting off green, it gradually turns purple, eventually maturing into a vibrant red colour. Throughout this ripening process, the pepper develops unique purple splotches, adding to its stunning looks. Plants are productive and reach around 90–120cm (3–4ft) tall. The peppers themselves can grow up to 6cm (2½in) in diameter, making them large enough for stuffing. Even though they look and smell like chillies, there is no perceptible heat to them.

Chillies

'Quickfire' F1 – This chilli is reported to be the quickest to crop from seed, but I love it for the tiny size of the plant, which only reaches 20cm (8in), if you're lucky. That said, the spicy little chillies are produced in their masses, with each plant having more than 100 fruits. Don't be fooled by the size of this plant, it's productive and the chillies are spicy, at SHU 40,000!

'Sugar Rush Stripey' – Perhaps one of the most attractive chillies out there, with candy cane stripes on twisted fruit. The orange and red stripes may look innocent, but this fruity flavoured chilli packs a punch. Plants can grow up to around 1m (3ft) in height, with the fruit starting off pale, then developing the stripes as it ripens. SHU 25,000–50,000.

'Buena Mulata' – Produces stunning fruit that start off almost metallic purple in colour! The shape is a traditional, cayenne, pointed chilli, with the flavour being comparable, but the fruit are so much prettier. Milder when purple, they will ripen through orange to a creamy colour, increasing in heat as they change. Plants grow to around 60–90cm (2–3ft) tall and are quite prolific, looking spectacular when covered in purple fruit. SHU 40,000.

'Scallywag' – An extraordinary new chilli pepper known for its exceptional hardiness, making it one of the most resilient varieties to grow. This Rocoto chilli pepper is also well suited to being grown as a perennial plant. Fuzzy leaves and vibrant purple flowers add an attractive element to this unusual plant, plus the seeds are jet black, rather than creamy

white. What sets this variety apart is its smaller fruit size, which ripens significantly earlier than its larger-fruited counterparts, so it is good for growing in the UK. It has a relaxed growth habit, making it particularly suitable for container gardening. Its cascading nature allows it to gracefully spill over the edges of pots or containers. I have successfully kept the same 'Scallywag' plant for several years by ensuring it remains frost-free during the winter months. Once spring arrives, it resumes growth, ready for another season. The fruit are thick and juicy, ideal to stuff with cream cheese, wrap in bacon and bake for a delicious extra-spicy treat. SHU 80,000.

'Peppapeach' – A paler version of the famed red Peppadew chilli from South Africa, normally found stuffed with cheese and preserved in oil. The creamy coloured chillies ripen from pale green and have a delicious spiciness and crisp flesh, perfect for stuffing or using in any recipe. The plants are productive, and the chillies have a mild, fruity flavour allowing them to be enjoyed raw in salads or salsa. SHU 1,000.

Problems

If flowers or buds drop from the plant, this is due to lack of water – as plants dry out, they abort their flowers and small fruit. So, if you see this happening, increase watering and make sure the plants are kept moist.

Holes in peppers can be caused by earwigs. If this is the case, you can trap them in newspaper before your peppers are damaged. Take a sheet of newspaper and roll it into a tube or roll it up like a sausage. Dampen the newspaper slightly to make it moist, then position it in your garden near the plants towards the end of the day. As night falls and earwigs become active, they will seek shelter within the dark and damp newspaper. Come morning, you have two options: either submerge the paper in a bucket of water, or dispose of it. You'll need to do this for several days to reduce the population of earwigs around your plants.

◄ 'Sugar Rush Stripey'

Cucumbers are one of those veggies that have a reputation for being a bit fiddly to grow, but fear not, with a little time and know-how, you can enjoy a bountiful harvest of fresh, juicy cucumbers all summer long, whether you have a greenhouse or not.

In the past, growing cucumbers successfully required lots of space and a heated greenhouse. However, thanks to some fantastic breeding breakthroughs in recent years, there are now cucumber varieties that can thrive just about anywhere. Some of these new varieties have no seeds, while others have thin skin that's easier to digest, meaning you're less likely to experience those pesky burps. Some cucumber seeds can be fairly expensive, but when you take into account the sheer number of fruit you get from one plant, especially if you opt for a smaller-fruited variety, they are good value. You will have more cucumbers than you know what to do with!

Traditionally, there were two main types of cucumbers: 'ridge' and 'greenhouse'. Ridge cucumbers were grown outdoors on raised mounds of soil, while greenhouse cucumbers were best suited for growing under cover. While some older varieties still follow these guidelines, many modern varieties can be grown both indoors and outdoors, so make sure you check the packet to see which conditions are suitable for your chosen variety. Personally, I'm a fan of growing smaller-fruited cucumber varieties in my garden. They produce plenty of bite-sized cucumbers that can be enjoyed in a single meal, without having to worry about half of a giant cucumber languishing in the fridge and going soft. Smaller cucumbers also tend to start cropping earlier than their larger counterparts, making them perfect for home gardening. And if you prefer something in between, there are even 'midi' fruited types that produce half-sized cucumbers. So, no matter what size you fancy, there's a cucumber variety out there for you to grow. You'll even find some varieties that are perfectly spherical, about the size of a golf ball.

How to grow

When it comes to starting your cucumber plants, the timing depends on where you plan to grow them. If you have a heated greenhouse, you can begin as early as late winter. For those growing in an unheated polytunnel or greenhouse, it's best to start in mid-spring. As for growing them outside, wait until mid to late spring before sowing, as cucumber plants grow rapidly and require a fair amount of space.

One important tip: hold off planting them outside until the weather is reasonably warm, usually in late spring. Cooler nights can potentially stunt or even kill your cucumber plants. By starting the seeds indoors, you reduce the risk of slug or snail damage, and you generally achieve better germination. Moreover, young seedlings are protected from inclement weather conditions.

However, if you prefer, you can directly sow the cucumber seeds outside. Just be sure to wait until late spring or ideally early summer, when the temperatures have warmed up. When sowing directly, I suggest planting three seeds in the same space. This accounts for the possibility of one seed being eaten by slugs, one seed being affected by unfavourable weather, and one seed successfully growing. If all three seeds survive, you'll need to thin them out and keep only the strongest seedling.

◀ Hanging basket cucumber 'Hopeline' F1

To provide extra protection and maintain a warmer environment, consider covering the seeds with a cloche or fleece during the first few weeks. This helps shield them from potential harm and keeps the area relatively warm during chilly nights.

Cucumber seeds are pretty large compared to most seeds, so it's best to start them in individual pots. You can choose to use a heated propagator or a sunny windowsill with a temperature of around 20–21°C (68–70°F). Personally, I find the 'half-pot' method works well for cucumber seedlings. Here's how it goes: take a 9–10cm (3½–4in) pot and fill it halfway with peat-free compost – this is important because cucumber seedlings tend to have a tall stem before the leaves emerge, making them a bit delicate and in need of support if started in a full pot. Next, sow the cucumber seed about 1–2cm (½–¾in) deep using the 'karate chop' technique. This means planting the seed on its edge, resembling your hand when you perform a karate chop, which allows water to easily run down the sides of the seed when you water the compost (rather than planting it flat side down and potentially making it rot). After sowing the seed, give the pot a good watering. Place it in a propagator or on a sunny windowsill and cover it with a plastic bag to maintain moisture in the compost.

After about a week or two, you'll see a seedling sprouting and starting to grow. Once the seedling has reached the top of the pot and the leaves have developed, you can carefully fill the rest of the pot with compost, covering the stem of the plant but leaving the leaves poking above the rim of the pot. By doing this, your cucumber plant will become sturdier and less prone to breakage. Additionally, it will encourage the development of more roots from the stem, resulting in a healthier plant with a stronger root system.

In my garden, I prefer to grow my cucumber plants outdoors up metal obelisks, to save space, but you can achieve the same effect by using cane or hazel poles that are approximately 1.8m (6ft) tall. Alternatively, you can allow your plants to ramble on a fence or trellis, or even let them spread over the ground. Just keep in mind that the fruit tends to attract slugs and snails, so it's a good idea to plant them through a membrane to keep the cucumbers off the soil.

When it comes to indoor growing, I find netting to be the most convenient support method. It works particularly well when secured to the roof of a greenhouse or the crossbars in a polytunnel. Not only does netting save space, it also effectively supports the weight of the developing fruit.

◄ Top row: seedlings in half pot and filling the pot with compost; Centre row: potting on cucumber seedlings and separatiing seedlings; Bottom row: transplating into bigger pots and watering newly transplanted seedlings

Top Tips

- If you are growing ridge cucumbers and you find the female flowers are falling off or the fruit is misshapen, this can be a result of poor pollination, usually earlier in the season, when there are fewer insects and cooler temperatures.

- If you want to grow seedless cucumbers, opt for a parthenocarpic variety; these types don't need insects to produce fruit and all the resulting fruit are seedless and sweet. These types are an excellent choice for growing in a heated greenhouse or for starting earlier in the season when there are no pollinators around. Keep them isolated from other cucumbers to ensure the fruit stays seedless.

- Consider using shading in the height of summer, which will prevent the plants scorching or wilting.

Most modern cucumber varieties have 'all-female' flowers, which means that each flower has a tiny fruit behind it. This tiny fruit will grow into a full-sized cucumber. Any flower that appears on a small stalk without the tiny fruit is a male flower and should be removed from the plant. Male flowers, if allowed to pollinate the other fruit, can cause them to taste bitter. It may sound a bit complicated, but it's quite simple: just keep the flowers with fruit behind them. Remember to pinch off the growing tips of the cucumber plants once they reach the roof of your greenhouse, otherwise you may end up with a tangled mass of overlapping shoots.

Outdoor (or ridge) cucumber varieties typically produce both male and female flowers, which require pollination to produce fruit. Therefore, make sure you leave all the flowers on these types of cucumbers.

They all benefit from regular liquid feedings, especially when flowers and fruit are developing. You can provide a weekly feed using homemade comfrey feed (see page 179) or tomato food. This will ensure healthy plants and generous harvests.

Harvesting and Storing

The timing of when to harvest depends on the variety you are growing, with smaller cucumbers usually ready before the longer ones. To ensure a clean break and to avoid damaging the plant, it's best to use a sharp knife or secateurs when cutting the fruit from the plant. Pulling the cucumbers can cause damage to either the fruit or the plant itself.

Keep a close eye on your cucumber plants and harvest the cucumbers as they become ripe, even if you don't immediately need them. Regular harvesting encourages a continuous supply. If you leave the fruit on the plant for too long, you may notice changes in colour, a bulging appearance or a soft texture; these are indications that the cucumbers are overripe and may not be suitable for eating.

After harvesting your cucumbers, you can help prolong their freshness by storing them in a plastic bag in the fridge, which will extend their shelf life and keep them crisp. Alternatively, if you've grown smaller cucumbers, you can pickle them or even create a delicious cucumber relish, which adds a delightful tangy flavour to burgers and other dishes.

So, remember to harvest your cucumbers when they are at their prime, handle them carefully, and consider various storage or preserving methods to make the most of your cucumber harvest!

Cucumbers to grow

'Merlin' – This is a midi type, producing 12–15cm (4½–6in) long fruit. It's an all-female variety, so it produces lots of fruit, with one or two cucumbers per leaf node. Although it's best grown under cover, it will crop outside too, plus it has fantastic disease resistance. Now that's magic!

'Bush Champion' – This 'non-climbing' type of cucumber is perfect for those looking for a compact and bushy plant. As the name implies, these plants typically reach a height of 25cm (10in) and spread out to around 90cm (3ft). Despite their smaller size, they are incredibly productive and begin bearing fruit early in the season. The cucumbers are approximately 25–30cm (10–12in) in length, boasting a crisp texture and great flavour. What's more, the plant's short and compact habit makes it an excellent choice for container gardening or even large baskets.

'Delistar' F1 – A thin-skinned variety, perfect for those who suffer from digestive issues after eating cucumber. The 16–18cm (6–7in) long fruit are deliciously sweet and crisp, plus the plants are very productive, with 50–100 fruits per plant not uncommon when grown in a greenhouse. If you're seeking a cucumber variety that is gentle on the stomach, yet still delivers a sweet and crunchy taste, then 'Delistar' F1 is an excellent option. Its thin skin and impressive productivity make it a top choice for greenhouse growing.

'Hopeline' F1 – A smaller-sized cucumber, reaching around 8–10cm (3–4in) long. The productive plants are great for growing inside, but also suitable for planting in pots or hanging baskets outside, where they will produce lots of crisp, refreshing fruit. I typically grow three plants in a 30cm (12in) wide, 20cm (8in) deep basket.

'Crystal Apple' – The flavour of these cucumbers is a treat for the tastebuds, as they are both sweet and juicy. When it's time to harvest, keep an eye on their colour transformation from green to vibrant lemon-yellow. This variety is suitable for outdoor growing in the UK, particularly in a sheltered spot where they can bask in full sun. Embrace its unique charm and enjoy its flavourful round fruits.

'Quick Snack' F1 – A compact variety perfect for indoor or windowsill growing, which can even be grown on a patio. It grows just 50–60cm (20–24in) tall but produces many small, crisp fruits (4–6cm/1½–2½in long). Being parthenocarpic, it doesn't need pollination, making it suitable for indoor growing.

The tiny, seedless cucumbers offer a hint of melon flavour and are great sliced lengthways in salads.

Problems

Bitter-tasting fruit occurs when plants experience stress, whether due to temperature extremes or inconsistent watering. If you notice bitter cucumbers on your plant, it's best to remove them, as it's likely that all the fruit will be affected. Take steps to address the underlying causes of stress: provide shading if the plants have been exposed to excessive heat and increase your watering routine. By addressing these issues, you can ensure that future fruit will be free from the unpleasant bitterness. Red spider mite can also affect cucumbers (see page 189).

(see page 189)

Top Tips

- It's beneficial to increase humidity in the greenhouse by dampening down the area with water during the day. This helps deter red spider mites, too, and will reduce the temperature, since cucumbers prefer temperatures below 25°C (77°F).

- Astound family and friends by using a cucumber mould to shape your cucumbers into star or heart shapes! Simply click the mould around small fruit and secure it to the plant. Then as the fruit grows and pushes against the mould, it transforms from cylindrical to shaped. You'll never see a star-shaped cucumber in the shops!!

◄ 'Quick Snack' F1
▼ Cucumbers from a cucumber mould

Tomatoes

Growing tomatoes at home offers a diverse array of options in terms of variety, colour and shape – which is why it's surprising that only red tomatoes are commonly found in stores. While red cherry tomatoes are most popular for purchase, home gardeners can easily produce green, orange, striped, blue and even black tomatoes. The darker-coloured varieties are known as 'antho' tomatoes, due to the colour coming from anthocyanin, the same pigment that makes blueberries blue. Modern breeding has led to some truly beautiful antho tomatoes, perfect for adding the wow factor to any salad. Contrary to popular belief, growing tomatoes in the UK doesn't necessarily require a greenhouse or polytunnel, as many varieties thrive in sunny outdoor locations during a typical British summer. When selecting the type of tomato plant to grow, it's essential to recognise that not all tomatoes develop in the same manner. There are two main growth habits: determinate (bush) and indeterminate (cordon or vine).

Determinate plants have a fixed height, which means they stop growing once they reach a specific size, then they focus their energy on ripening the fruit they've produced. Most of the fruit typically ripens within a short span of a few weeks, with some varieties cropping again after several weeks. These plants are often referred to as bush tomatoes, producing smaller plants ranging from 20cm (8in) to 1m (3ft) in height. Micro-toms, the smallest varieties, can thrive in a pot as small as 15cm (6in) wide and are perfect for growing on a sunny windowsill or on a shelf in the greenhouse. Hanging-basket tomatoes and container-growing varieties are also categorised as determinate plants, although some larger types may need support to prevent the weight of the ripening fruit causing the plant to collapse.

Indeterminate plants, also known as cordon or vine tomatoes, continue growing as long as the weather permits. However, they should be limited to a height of 1.8–2m (6–6$\frac{1}{2}$ft) in our gardens, which is the standard greenhouse height, but also because it allows the fruit to ripen on the plant without leaving too many unripe tomatoes at the end of the season. It is generally best to limit your plants to 5–7 trusses of fruit on a cordon plant, which will ensure they all ripen before cooler weather slows their growth. These plants are typically trained up canes, strings or other supports, with side shoots removed to create a tall, slender plant that bears fruit from the main stem. As a result, they are better suited for indoor growing, where they are protected from strong winds that could snap or topple them. However, if grown against a south-facing fence or wall, many smaller-fruited varieties will successfully produce fruit in an average summer.

When it comes to choosing which tomato varieties to grow, just keep in mind that not all tomatoes are created equal! So, after figuring out where you'll grow them and which type to go for, ask yourself, 'What am I going to use these tomatoes for?' Are you craving some sweet, tiny tomatoes to snack on while you're wandering around your garden? Or maybe you fancy those big beefsteak tomatoes that are perfect for pairing with mozzarella and basil? Or you might want some fleshy, savoury plums for whipping up your own pasta sauce. Most small cherry tomatoes are just perfect for snacking and salads because they're sweeter, but they can make a soup or sauce a bit too sweet; and while many plum and paste tomatoes might not taste like much when they're raw, when you cook them they transform into a luscious, thick sauce without any trouble (since they're fleshy with few seeds). So whatever

▶ Hanging basket tomatoes

you choose, remember that each type has its own special uses, which can save you ending up with super-sweet sauces when you use cherry tomatoes or being disappointed by bland plum tomatoes in your salad.

With the many varieties and colours available to grow at home, you can easily produce a summer's worth of tasty, colourful home-grown tomatoes no matter the size of your growing space.

How to grow

If you have access to grow lights and a heated greenhouse, tomato seeds can be started as early as mid-winter. However, if you don't have these facilities, it's better to wait until early spring to start greenhouse varieties and mid-spring for outdoor varieties. To sow the seeds, place them on the surface of moist, peat-free compost, and cover them with a thin layer of compost.

Tomatoes require warmth to germinate, so it's advisable to keep them in a heated propagator or on a sunny windowsill covered with a plastic bag until the seedlings emerge. Once the seedlings have produced two true leaves, it's time to transplant them into individual pots. When doing this, plant the seedlings deeply as they will produce more roots from the lower part of the stem if they are covered in compost, resulting in a stronger plant.

To transplant, you can either plant the seedling straight down into a prepared hole or bend the lower part of the stem into a U shape to allow for planting up to its first leaves, after removing the seed leaves. Depending on when you started your seeds, you may need to pot them up again before moving them to an unheated greenhouse.

When transplanting, I use a 15cm (6½in) pot and remove the bottom leaves of the plant to prevent them being covered in compost. Although it may seem unusual, this method increases the number of roots the plant will produce, while also encouraging the flowers and fruit to grow lower on the plant. This is especially beneficial for a domestic greenhouse, where you want the fruit to be as low on the plant as possible to maximise the number of trusses of fruit you can fit within a limited height of around 2m (6½ft).

When your plants are finally moved to their growing space in an unheated greenhouse, you'll need to provide something for cordon types to be trained up – this can be twine, canes or poles. As the plants grow, they will need tying in loosely to stop the upper stems flopping – secure them underneath any developing fruit truss, which can become heavy and will need extra support. They should be planted 30–45cm (12–18in) apart, depending on the type you are growing.

To remove side shoots from cordon-style tomato plants, pluck off any developing shoots emerging from the leaf axis. If they are too thick to remove by hand, you may use secateurs. A helpful tip is to visualise the tomato plant as a person standing upright with arms extended, then remove any growth emerging from the area between the shoulder and neck. By removing these side shoots, the plant can focus on producing fruit instead of excess leaves. In contrast, bush-type tomatoes require no side shooting and can be left to grow naturally.

Establishing a regular routine for watering and feeding your tomato plants is crucial for promoting healthy growth and the tastiest tomatoes. Consistent care will result in larger plants and the highest-quality tomatoes. Failure to water your plants regularly can cause them to wilt, and it can also lead to blossom end rot (see page 167), a condition characterised by dark, sunken patches on the base of developing fruit.

In addition to regular watering, I would recommend feeding your plants once a week using either homemade comfrey feed or a high-potash liquid fertiliser. It's best to begin this routine once the first small, green tomatoes appear on your plants.

When your greenhouse tomato plants have grown to the point where they have reached the roof or are 1.8–2m (6–6½ft) in height and have produced 5–7 trusses of fruit, it's time to 'top' them. Topping involves removing the top of the plant down to the last leaf. This practice can help prevent the plant growing taller and instead encourage it to channel its energy into ripening its fruit.

Grafted tomato plants are gaining popularity for growing at home due to their enhanced productivity and resilience. These plants are formed by joining a robust and disease-resistant rootstock onto a

▶ Top left: tomato seedlings; top right: separating seedlings; Centre left: transplating seedlings deeply; Centre right: transplanting seedling using the 'U' method; Bottom left: firming in seedlings; Bottom right: watering seedlings; Far right: harvested comfrey leaves

Top Tips

- If you are left with lots of green tomatoes, put them in a paper bag with a ripe banana; the ethylene gas released by the banana will help to ripen the tomatoes.

- If you grow comfrey, you can use it to nourish your tomato plants in two ways. First, you can produce comfrey 'tea', which functions as a type of plant food, by chopping up the leaves and letting them break down into a smelly brown liquid in a sealed container of water. The finished liquid can be watered over plants diluted to a rate of one part comfrey to 10 parts water. Alternatively, you can shred the leaves and spread a layer approximately 2cm (¾in) deep around your plants. This will rapidly dry out and transform into a 'crumb' that can help fertilise your plants as you water them, with the water gradually dissolving the nutrients from the comfrey. This is a far easier, and less smelly way to feed them.

delicious top tomato variety, resulting in a fusion of two seedlings into one robust plant. This technique is similar to grafting apples, where the rootstock dictates the growth of the plant. Grafted tomato plants can produce up to 75 per cent more fruit per plant, thrive in cooler growing conditions, and exhibit stronger resistance to diseases. The beauty of this process is that it is entirely natural, with no chemicals or glues involved, as nature skilfully merges the two plants together.

Harvesting and storing

Tomatoes can be harvested individually or as a cluster when they are fully ripe. Solid-coloured tomatoes are the easiest to identify as they will have an even colour and a slight softness when gently squeezed. Some varieties have a built-in release mechanism (elbow) above the calyx (the sepals beneath the flower or fruit) that can be pressed to easily remove the fruit from the plant, which is great when harvesting with one hand. However, larger-fruited varieties may need to be cut from the plant to avoid damage.

Tomatoes with multiple colours, or antho types, can be trickier to determine when they are ripe, particularly if they are mainly black in colour. Harvesting too early can result in green, tasteless tomatoes. To avoid this, check the bottom of the fruit and under the calyx by gently lifting it. If the colour has changed or turned red, it is ready to be harvested. After harvesting, store tomatoes at room temperature to fully develop their flavour. Though they can be refrigerated, it is best to remove them at least an hour before eating to allow the flavours to develop.

If you have an abundance of tomatoes, there are various ways to store them. You can make sauces or soups and freeze or bottle them. Alternatively, dehydrate them either in an oven or using a dehydrator (there are plenty of instructions online) until they become chewy, like gummy sweets, then store them in jars of oil and vinegar with some herbs. This makes them a great addition to salads, pasta, soups or for snacking; it is one of my favourite ways to preserve my harvest, as every time I open a jar I'm taken back to warm summer days in the greenhouse. Freezing the whole fruit is the easiest way to store them for cooking purposes. Simply lay the clean fruit on a tray, freeze until solid, and transfer into a freezer-safe container. Thaw before using; the skin can easily be removed if desired.

◄ Top left: how to harvest using the elbow release; Top right: removing side shoots; Bottom left: rooting side shoots in water; Bottom right: side shoots ready to root

Top Tips

- Large-fruited varieties may need additional support for heavy trusses. You can support them with string tied to the plant, or you can 'truss prune' them, which involves removing several of the developing fruit from each truss, enabling the plant to support them without the stem kinking or snapping.

- An economical way to grow more tomato plants is to allow the side shoots to grow up to 10–15cm (4–6in) in length, detach them from the parent plant, and place them in a glass of water until they develop roots. Once rooted, these shoots can be potted and grown into new plants – perfect if you are growing varieties that only have 4–5 seeds per packet and you want more plants for free.

- If it's not warm enough to plant cordon-type tomatoes in an unheated greenhouse and they are becoming too tall, let them start to produce side shoots and don't remove them. This will slow your plants' vertical growth, so you can remove the shoots when you finally plant them out.

- Tomatoes are self-pollinating, meaning even if you only grow one plant you will get tomatoes. The flowers have both male and female parts, with the transfer of pollen taking place within one flower. However, to ensure all the flowers produce fruit it's a good idea to gently shake the plants when you pass them, ensuring the pollen gets where it needs to go!

Tomatoes to grow

When it comes to recommending which varieties to grow, there are so many to choose from; these are some of my favourites.

Indeterminate

'Gargamel' – This red, gold and black-streaked antho tomato is simply beautiful! It is named after the fictional wizard in the hit TV cartoon The Smurfs, because of the similar colours to his robe. Not only that, it's also got a great taste and always attracts comments when cut into wedges for a salad. The round- to plum-shaped fruit weigh around 100–120g (3½–4½oz), with a sweet tomato flavour.

'Black Moon' F1 ('Two Tasty' in the US) – This F1 hybrid is a new two-tone, two-bite-sized, red cherry tomato with black antho shoulders. Sweet and savoury tasting, this attractive variety has come top in international taste tests, beating previous winners such as 'Sungold'. It's another attractive tomato that not only looks great, but has the flavour to match, plus it has some resistance to late blight. The slightly elongated fruit weigh 30–40g (1–1½oz) each.

'Honeycomb' F1 – A beautiful, golden-orange, cherry-sized fruit that has a deep sweetness reminiscent of honey. When ripe, the tomatoes have a fruity juiciness to them which works well in salads and for snacking. Resistant to the skin splitting, which makes it the ultimate choice for those who love 'Sungold' but want a less problematic tomato to grow.

'Red Currant' – Not only the smallest tomato fruit in the world, it's also a different species to traditional garden varieties. Discovered on a Peruvian beach in 1707, it's distinct from the typical garden tomato and has remained largely unchanged since then. These plants boast exceptional disease resistance and can withstand cooler temperatures. The small tomatoes they produce are bursting with a delightful sweet and tangy taste, making them a great addition to salads or for snacking straight off the vine. Expect bowls full of tiny fruit all summer.

'Berkeley Tie Dye' – A unique and visually striking variety that originated in Berkeley, California. They are medium to large in size and have a beefsteak shape with a flattened appearance. Their skin is a blend of green, purple and red hues, creating a distinctive tie-dye pattern, while the flesh inside is a mix of red and green, with a sweet and tangy flavour that is highly praised by tomato enthusiasts. Perfect for slicing and adding to sandwiches, salads or enjoying on their own.

◄ Top left: 'Blaue Zimmertomate'; Top right: 'Black Moon' F1; Bottom left: 'Gargamel'; Bottom right: 'Romello' F1

Top Tips

- When removing leaves from tomatoes, save them to make an anti-pest spray. Using tomato-leaf spray is a great way to tackle aphids and mites on your plants, and it's all thanks to the alkaloids in the leaves that can be deadly to many types of pests. Take 2 cups of chopped tomato leaves, soak them in 450ml (15fl oz) of water overnight, and strain the liquid the next day while getting rid of the leaves onto the compost heap. Then, add another 450ml (15fl oz) of water to the solution and give your plants a good spray. Bye-bye bugs!

- If starting seeds on a windowsill, remember it can become cold at night behind curtains or blinds, so move your seedlings in the evening, placing them back on the windowsill in the morning.

'Vivacious' F1 – Radiant orange-red fruits that offer an ideal blend of flavour and nutrition, containing high levels of beta-carotene in a single tomato that's equivalent to 40 per cent of the recommended daily intake of vitamin A. These 7–8cm (2¾–3in) oval-shaped tomatoes boast a meaty yet juicy texture and a well-balanced taste with a harmonious mix of sweetness and acidity. Each plant will produce around 70 fruits and is tolerant of late blight.

Determinate

'Romello' F1 – A highly acclaimed variety of mini plum tomato that grows into a sizeable and bushy plant, to a width of up to 90cm (3ft). This productive plant is perfect for growing in containers, large baskets or in the ground, yielding an impressive 5kg (11lb) of fruit throughout the season. Additionally, the fruit grows on the exterior of the plant, making harvesting a breeze. With resistance to late blight, this tomato variety is easy to grow.

'Orangeto' F1 – A low-maintenance tomato variety that produces lots of small, bright orange, cherry-sized fruit. These sweet and delectable tomatoes are grown on a sizeable and bushy plant, making them perfect for half-barrels or growing in the garden. They can even be left to sprawl, acting as a ground-cover plant while still offering a bountiful harvest of 35–40g (1¼–1½oz) fruits. Additionally, it's resistant to late blight, providing gardeners with a robust and reliable crop.

'Veranda Red' F1 – A compact and bushy tomato plant, standing at only 30cm (12in) tall, yet offering the bold and flavourful taste of a vine tomato. Perfect for smaller containers and baskets, this variety can even be grown in pots as small as 11cm (4in) wide. A true British-bred tomato, it is well suited to outdoor growing in the UK, with a resistance to late blight. This fast-growing tomato variety can be sown as late as late spring and still yield an abundant crop.

'Sunny Drops Orange' F1 – Produces tear-drop-shaped orange fruit on a small plant that only reaches around 30cm (12in) tall – ideal for growing on a windowsill. I love to grow these in small pots on the shelves in my greenhouse, as they make one of the best semi-dried tomatoes for storing in oil and vinegar. Not only is it tasty, but this attractive tomato also grows well in lower light conditions and produces its fruit on the outside of the plant, meaning harvesting is easy.

'Blaue Zimmertomate' – One of the smallest antho varieties you can grow, producing lots of 20g (¾oz) red and black fruit on tiny plants that only reach

30–35cm (12–14in) tall. Sweet and tangy, the fruit look stunning, almost like jewels adorning this pot-perfect-sized plant.

Blight-resistant varieties

With blight becoming more of an issue for those of us who want to grow tomatoes outside, there are blight-resistant varieties now more widely available for us to grow at home, notably 'Crimson Crush' F1, 'Cocktail Crush' F1, 'Rubylicious' F1, 'Consuelo' F1, 'Nagina' F1 and 'Rose Crush' F1.

Problems

Blossom end rot is typically caused by a calcium deficiency, causing the base of the fruit to become black and sunken. The problem isn't usually caused by lack of calcium in the compost or soil, but by the fact that the plant can't take up the calcium due to irregular or lack of watering. Affected fruit are best composted, and watering of the plants should be increased to help prevent the problem recurring.

Late blight is a destructive disease caused by a fungal-like pathogen that can completely ruin tomato plants within just a few days after initial infection. The disease can affect every part of the plant, with the leaves typically showing the first visible signs of infection by developing dark patches and then rapidly collapsing and shrivelling. Stems can also display dark lesions, and fruit may develop a leathery appearance. The entire plant can ultimately collapse within 48 hours. Blight is typically spread through water droplets, making outdoor plants more susceptible to infection. There are now many blight-resistant tomato varieties available, but even these may still display 10–15 per cent damage from blight. However, they can survive and continue to grow through the disease rather than dying. When watering tomato plants, it's crucial to water the soil directly and avoid getting water on the plant itself. If your plants are affected by blight, it's essential to remove and dispose of them properly by burning or discarding them instead of composting them, to avoid spreading the disease.

▶ Top left: 'Orangeto' F1; top right: 'Akoya' F1; Bottom left: 'Rebel Starfighter Prime'; Bottom right: 'Sunny Drops Orange' F1

Aubergines

While some call them aubergines, others know them as eggplants or brinjal. Whichever term you use, these large purpley-black vegetables were once predominantly used for dishes like moussaka and are the primary type available in shops. However, there is now a diverse range of aubergine varieties that can be grown at home. They come in an array of colours, such as white, green, violet and striped, as well as various shapes from sausage-like forms to those resembling the size and shape of a ping-pong ball. Additionally, there are new varieties with dwarf growing habits, which are ideal for growing on windowsills or on a shelf in the greenhouse, making it possible to enjoy a touch of Mediterranean flavour regardless of your location and climate. While older varieties can produce quite a few spines on the midrib of leaves and around the neck of the fruit, more modern ones are smooth and spine-free, making them easier to grow and harvest.

Growing aubergines can be challenging, as these heat-loving plants need an early start to produce a good harvest. This can be difficult without access to heat and grow lights so, considering this, you might want to opt for a smaller-sized variety that can grow and crop within the limited summer months or buy a plant from a mail-order company or garden centre, preferably a grafted one. Grafted aubergines can begin producing fruit up to two months earlier than their non-grafted counterparts, and they exhibit increased vigour and adaptability to cooler temperatures, making them perhaps the best grafted vegetable plant there is.

However, if you have a heated propagator to start your seeds into growth and a greenhouse for nurturing the plants, you can explore a variety of intriguing aubergine options. While I personally adore moussaka made with my own aubergines, the smaller varieties are great for enhancing the flavours of soups and curries. The elongated aubergines can be roasted or grilled on the barbecue, then served alongside lamb and a fresh salad, making for a truly delectable meal!

How to grow

Like many Mediterranean vegetables, aubergines need warmth to germinate. It's worth considering a small, heated propagator or heat mat to provide an optimal temperature of 15–20°C (59–68°F) for germination. Alternatively, you can use an airing cupboard and then transfer seedlings to a light windowsill once they sprout, or try a windowsill, although cooler temperatures may result in lower germination rates. To allow for a lengthy growing season, seeds can be sown in mid-winter if you have access to heat and lights; otherwise, waiting until late winter is recommended. Seeds can be started in modules or trays with a 0.5cm (¼in) layer of peat-free compost on top, and they should germinate within 2–3 weeks.

Once seedlings develop their first true leaves, transplant them into individual pots and continue to grow them until the threat of frost has passed, which typically occurs between late spring and early summer in most parts of the UK. At this point, transfer them to 30cm (12in) pots or plant them in the border, spacing them about 40–45cm (16–18in) apart. If you're growing larger-fruited varieties, consider adding sturdy canes for support as the ripening fruit starts to weigh down the plants.

Keep in mind that different aubergine varieties can vary in height from 40cm (16in) to 2m (6½ft), so check the specific variety before sowing. Some highly productive types are available but may require more space. If the plants you are growing are tall ones, nip the growing tip of the main stem when it reaches 30cm (12in) tall, as this will encourage it to produce a bushier plant with more fruit.

To help keep plants well watered, you can mulch around the base with a thick layer of well-rotted manure or garden compost – this should also prevent too many weeds growing around your plants. Then, once the flowers begin to form, water the plants with a high-potassium liquid fertiliser such as a good-quality tomato feed, or your own homemade comfrey tea (see page 179).

As your plants produce fruit, limit larger-fruited varieties to 5–6 per plant by removing any new flowers, while smaller-fruited ones can be left to produce many more. However, if you are growing a grafted plant you can leave 10–12 large fruit on the plant as long as you remove smaller ones towards the end of summer – this allows the larger ones to ripen.

Harvesting and storing

No matter the shape and colour of the aubergines you're growing, they should always be harvested when they are plump and shiny, as this is a sign they are ripening, before the colour starts to change, when the seeds inside will be tough and the flesh can become bitter. Using sharp secateurs, cut the fruit from the plant, being careful not to catch yourself on any spines they may have. Never try to pull fruit from the plant, as they are simply too tough for that to work. Aubergines can also become bitter-tasting if they have been picked a few days previously and not eaten straight away. You can remove the bitterness by slicing the fruit and sprinkling with salt to draw out some of the water and the bitter compounds, then rinse and pat dry before using them. If you are preparing a lot of fruit in one go, remember to brush the cut slices with lemon juice to prevent them from oxidising and going brown, or grow a variety that is slow to discolour. Certain types of aubergine, like the long, sausage-shaped ones, can have quite a few seeds in them, although they will become tender and unnoticeable when cooked.

I always pick and use the fruit from my plants as soon as it's ready, which sometimes means there is a glut to process in the kitchen. Slicing your aubergines into 1cm (½in) thick strips and griddling them is a great way to use them up; they can then be added cold to salads, or frozen for use later. You can also chop them into chunks and roast them with garlic and herbs, again freezing them for use later with other Mediterranean veg or to add to soups and stews, where they will soften and become lusciously silky. You can even preserve your aubergines in oil to create your own antipasto – perfect for platters and adding to pasta.

Aubergines to grow

'Meatball' F1 – This fatter-fruited variety has dense flesh which is very slow to oxidise, so it won't go brown like shop-bought aubergines. It also has sweeter, firmer flesh, with fewer seeds, making it a great choice to slice and griddle for a meat-free veggie steak.

'Jackpot' F1 – A spine-free, dwarf variety that only reaches 55–60cm (22–24in) tall and is covered in small aubergines for a long cropping period. Ideal for growing in containers, and particularly suited to those who don't have much space.

'Green Knight' F1 – Produces slender, jade-green aubergines on large plants that can reach 1.5m (5ft) or more; it's best to use canes or poles as support for the copious amount of fruit produced. Ideal for slicing, this variety is not only beautiful to look at but also delicious in stir-fries or curries.

'Pinstripe' F1 – A nearly spine-free, dense variety that produces an abundant harvest of dark purple fruits adorned with unique white stripes. The eye-catching fruits and compact, dwarf nature of the plant make this perfect for sunny patios or compact greenhouses and vegetable gardens.

'Scorpio' F1 (grafted plants only) – This super-productive variety has yielded 21 fruits on just one of my plants, making it by far the biggest cropper out of all the aubergines I've grown. Almost spine-free, the fruit are the traditional shape and black colour, with a mild taste. If you love aubergine but only have the space for one plant, this is the one to grow.

Problems

Red spider mite is perhaps the biggest problem to contend with when growing aubergines at home. These tiny insects are hard to see with the naked eye, and usually they are only noticed when the plant's leaves start to yellow and the tell-tale webbing the pests produce is visible around the leaves. They don't like humid atmospheres, so spraying the floor of the greenhouse a couple of times a day can help lessen the problem, and you can also buy beneficial insects which are housed in little sachets you hang from the plants to get rid of the pest.

Whitefly can be a problem on aubergines in the greenhouse, but you can use Nicotiana, or tobacco plants, as a decoy. Plant them by the door of your greenhouse, outside, then when they start to show signs of whitefly infestation you can spray them with a weak sugar-water solution – this sticks the insects to the plants and allows you to remove the plant along with the pests and add it to the compost. To make the solution, simply mix 5 teaspoons of sugar with a mug of boiling water (I usually do this when I'm making my morning cuppa), then allow it to cool and use when needed.

▶ Top: Red spider mite on aubergine leaves; Bottom: aubergine flower

In terms of low-maintenance vegetables, squash, pumpkins and courgettes (zucchini) certainly rank highly! I love to grow a selection for use in the warmer months that will store all winter, giving me a reminder of summer when I decide to turn one into a mouthwatering meal.

These heat-loving plants are not only simple to grow but also extremely fruitful, offering a variety of shapes, sizes and growing styles that can accommodate any garden or growing area. Courgettes and summer squashes yield an abundance of tender, sweet fruits, ideal for grilling, incorporating into pasta sauces or adding to salads when small. On the other hand, pumpkins and winter squashes are better suited for long-term storage and shine soups, roasted dishes or even pies – for instance, a 'Crown Prince' squash makes a pumpkin pie taste even better!

As for distinguishing between pumpkins and winter squash, pumpkins typically have a larger, rounder shape and a sizeable central seed cavity, making them a popular choice for Halloween carving. The seed cavity can be quite fibrous, and the flesh may be more watery. Conversely, winter squash exhibit a variety of shapes, colours and sizes, featuring a smaller seed cavity and firmer, more flavourful flesh with fewer fibrous strands surrounding the seeds. This makes them simpler to hollow out and prepare. There is even a particular squash variety with a distinct flesh that when scraped with a fork after cooking separates into strands, creating an excellent gluten-free pasta substitute. This squash is fittingly called a 'Spaghetti' squash. Both winter squash and pumpkins can be stored for an extended period if kept in a cool, dry environment, but pumpkins, particularly those with thinner skins, generally have a shorter shelf life than most winter squash.

Summer squash refers to a broad category of squash varieties harvested during the summer months when they are still immature, which results in tender and edible skin. Courgettes are a specific type of summer squash and are a favourite among gardeners, not only for their ease in growing, but for the copious amount of fruit they bear. Summer squash varieties exhibit considerable variation in terms of shape, size and colour. Courgettes generally have a cylindrical shape, almost like a sausage, and their colours can be green, yellow or striped. Other summer squash types may be round, flat or curved, with colours spanning from green to yellow or even a mix of both. Patty pan squash, for example, are especially well-liked for their distinctive, UFO-like shape and they are delicious sautéed when small or hollowed out and stuffed when a bit bigger.

When deciding which pumpkin or squash variety to grow, the space you have available should be a key factor, as some vining types can sprawl 3–4m (10–13ft) from their planting site. However, you can train these plants to grow vertically by attaching them to arches, obelisks or fences, which helps maximise your space and yield an abundant harvest. Just be sure to choose a variety with smaller fruits and make sure the supporting structure is robust, as the weight of the fruits can easily topple a weak growing frame.

Pumpkins and Squash

◄ 'Crown Prince'

Although pumpkins and winter squash can yield a decent harvest or even exceptionally large fruits on occasion, it's the courgette that stands out as a prolific producer, with just one or two plants usually sufficing for an average family. Many gardeners have experienced planting too many, and resorted to leaving the excess on the doorsteps of unsuspecting friends and neighbours. It's almost a gardening rite of passage to be amazed by their impressive productivity, as well as the speed at which a small fruit can transform into a gigantic one!

It's well worth growing a couple of plants if you have the space, and again, smaller-fruited varieties can easily be trained up a fence, obelisk or even wires on a wall. This not only maximises your growing space, it also allows you to grow more unusual types that you can't find for sale in the shops.

How to grow

Pumpkins and squashes thrive in warm, sunny conditions, so avoid planting them in shady areas where they may not perform as well. Also, remember that they grow really quickly, and starting seeds indoors too early may lead to large plants that overtake the windowsill before they can be transplanted.

It's best to start seeds indoors from mid-spring, allowing for a healthy-sized plant ready for transplanting into the garden four weeks later. Seeds should be sown direct from late spring. Though this may seem late, the plants will catch up quickly and benefit from warmer soil temperatures. However, slugs and snails are drawn to these plants, so starting them indoors and transplanting seedlings is more reliable.

When sowing large seeds, keep in mind the 'karate chop' position, meaning the seed should be placed on its side, like a hand chopping downwards. This reduces the risk of seed rot, as excess water will run down the sides instead of pooling on the surface.

Sow one seed per 9cm (3½in) pot for a healthy seedling within a couple of weeks. For outdoor-sown seeds, place two per station and thin to the healthiest one. When transplanting outdoors, remember these plants are heavy feeders, so incorporate plenty of compost or well-rotted manure into the bed beforehand and ensure consistent watering for best results.

Spacing depends on the plant type: bush-sized courgettes and squash should be approximately 90cm (3ft) apart, while trailing or 'vining' types require at least 2m (6½ft) between them to prevent entanglement and confusion as to which plant is which. For larger plants that become unwieldy or grow in undesired directions, use a stick pushed into the soil to guide the vine the way you want it to grow, or prune the vine's tip to halt growth. This encourages side shoot growth for a wider, more productive plant, plus the pruned tip can be cooked like spinach or chard and eaten!

Harvesting and storing

Pick and consume summer squash, patty pan and courgettes as they grow. Smaller fruits are sweeter and more tender, allowing the tiniest to be sliced thinly and eaten raw in salads, while larger ones can become watery, tasteless and fibrous. To make sure plants keep cropping, continually harvest the fruit, even if you don't need it; otherwise, allowing them to grow too large may inhibit new fruit development. Share any excess with friends and family to ensure a consistent supply of smaller, tender fruits; although be warned, there are only so many that people will accept before they have had their fill. I find leaving a bag of courgettes on the doorstep, then knocking on the door and making a speedy getaway enables you to get rid of excess fruit without the fear of anyone politely declining your offer! When harvesting, cut the fruit from the plant, as twisting or pulling may damage or uproot it. Watch out for small spines on the stems, which can damage the fruit and scratch your skin.

Winter squashes and pumpkins are typically harvested around mid-autumn just before the first frost, allowing them to grow and 'cure'. Curing refers to the fruit's skin ripening and hardening, which enables longer storage throughout winter and spring months. Depending on the fruit size, limit the number of plants to two or three large pumpkins or up to 10 small squashes. Retain only perfect fruit on the plant, as damaged ones will not store well and will draw energy away from it ripening other fruits. By late summer, remove any flowers and small fruits from winter squash and pumpkins, as they won't have time to develop into viable fruit and may hinder the growth of other fruits.

If plants are growing on the ground, place the fruit on a brick or tile to prevent the base rotting on damp soil and to aid in curing the skin by absorbing the sun's heat. Encourage this further by removing any shading leaves, allowing the fruit to sit in full sun to harden the skin and ripen the flesh.

When harvesting, take a T-section of the vine along with the squash or pumpkin handle, as this prevents rot from spreading to the fruit and reducing the storage life. Store fruit in a frost-free, cool area away from direct sunlight to maximise the length of time that they will keep, with some lasting until the following spring, if stored correctly.

◀ Top left: planting climbing courgette; Top right: tying in climbing courgette; Bottom left: removing leaves that shade fruit; Bottom right: placing fruit on a tile to cure

Top Tips

- When planting, push a stick or bamboo cane in next to the plant, then you will know where to water most effectively once the large leaves become a mass of green.

- It's not just the fruit and flowers that are edible, leaves and stems of squash and courgettes can also be eaten and are a favourite dish in many African countries. They may seem unappetising because of the small hairs, however, when blanched or cooked in butter with garlic the hairs dissolve and the result is a spinach-like dish which is delicious!

- Never lift large squash or pumpkin by the handle of the fruit as it can snap off, resulting in it not lasting in storage. Instead, always lift from the bottom of the fruit.

- You can create your own bird feed by washing, drying and roasting squash and pumpkin seeds – the perfect way to use something you would otherwise compost.

- Lack of fruit, or small fruit dropping from the plant, can be a result of pollination issues. For fruit to develop, there must have been pollination from a male flower to a female one, and early in the season when there are fewer pollinating insects this can be a problem. Take a male flower from the plant and press it around a female flower to aid pollination.

Pumpkins and squash to grow

Summer squash

'Tromboncino' (vining) – Similar to a butternut squash but picked when it's still tender and green. This squash tastes like a sweeter type of courgette and has a long, seedless neck, which makes it ideal for preparing and cooking. For long, straight fruit you are best to grow these vining plants vertically, with one plant producing around six big squashes.

'Sunburst' (bush) – This bright yellow, patty-pan-type squash produces lots of flying-saucer-shaped fruit from a bush-type plant, perfect to grow in the ground or a large container. Small fruit can be harvested and cooked on the barbecue as kebabs, or thinly sliced and served in salads for a nutty, crisp addition. Fruit can be allowed to get to saucer size, then hollowed out and stuffed with rice or meat before baking.

'Sure Thing' (bush) – A traditional, green-coloured courgette with a difference – it's self-fertile and needs no insects to produce fruit, which makes it the ideal variety to grow in a tunnel or earlier in the season when there may be fewer pollinating insects around. The only courgette to crop no matter the weather, plus it's the perfect bush-sized plant.

'Black Forest' and 'Shooting Star' (vining) – These green and yellow climbing courgettes can be tied into supports and grown vertically, saving space while maximising your harvest. Growing them as climbing plants makes harvesting easier, and the fruit are less susceptible to slug and snail damage at a young age.

Winter squash and pumpkins

'Honeyboat' (vining) – Perhaps my favourite winter squash, with green and cream stripes that fade as it stores, so you know which to eat first as the green stripes change to orange, essentially creating an inbuilt best-before-date indicator! Sweet-flavoured and smooth-textured, no wonder it earned the nickname 'sweet potato squash'; plus the skin is edible and becomes crisp and chewy when baked, just like a baked potato! The squashes are the ideal size for two people and plants can be grown on the floor or up supports as the fruit aren't too heavy. Stores very well.

'Crown Prince' (vining) – This steel-blue winter squash is one of the best known and tastiest squashes available to grow at home, with yellow-orange, sweet-tasting flesh. Perfect to use in any pumpkin pie recipe, these 3–4kg (6½–8¾lb) squash will keep you in scrumptious soup all winter long. Stores well.

'Butterbush' F1 (bush) – A compact, small-fruited butternut squash which is ideal for smaller spaces or containers. The fruit reach around 800g–1kg (1¾–2¼lb) and you can expect 3–6 per small plant. The fruit also ripen earlier in the season, meaning you're certain to get a crop even if the weather takes a turn for the worse at the end of the season.

'Spaghetti' (vining) – This unassuming, rugby-ball-shaped squash comes into its own when cut in half and baked; it produces spaghetti-like strands when the flesh is scooped out with a fork. This gluten-free vegetable spaghetti can be used for any recipe that requires traditional pasta, yet has a fraction of the calories. The fruit also store well through winter.

'Triple Treat' (vining) – This is a pumpkin that does it all – you can carve the large orange fruit for Halloween, but don't forget to save the hull-less seeds as they can be baked for a tasty snack without the need to remove the fiddly seed shells before eating. The flesh of this variety is also tasty and smooth-textured, unlike other carving types, which are tasteless. Therefore, no matter what you want to grow a pumpkin for, this one does it all!

Problems

Lack of female (fruiting) flowers can be an issue for pumpkin and squash plants. (Female flowers are the ones with tiny fruit behind the bloom, while male ones lack this.) This problem usually occurs early in the season when night-time temperatures are lower, or when plants aren't watered enough. Consider sowing and planting a couple of weeks later, or covering plants with horticultural fleece. Make sure plants are in full sun, as shade can stress the plants.

Bitter-tasting fruit is normally the result of growing plants from saved seed that cross-pollinated with another squash, producing a bitter-tasting chemical that can cause stomach ache. Affected plants should be composted and any saved seed disposed of.

Powdery mildew is a problem that most squash and pumpkins suffer from as the season progresses and the weather gets warmer and drier. The dusty white coating on the leaves is a tell-tale sign, so remove the leaves immediately, as this will slow the spread. Stressed and cramped plants suffer worse, so make sure to keep them well watered and mulched, with plenty of space between them. You can also spray plants with a product called 'SB Plant Invigorator' at the first sign of problems, as this non-chemical mildew control can help slow the spread and give your plants longer to produce their harvest.

▲ Top left: 'Honeyboat'; Top right: 'Tromboncino'; Bottom left: 'Sunburst'; Bottom right: 'Black Forest'

Index

Writing a book is a remarkable journey that involves the support and assistance of numerous individuals, both directly and indirectly. It's difficult to imagine this book being in your hands without the collective help and encouragement I received along the way.

First and foremost, I owe a tremendous debt of gratitude to my grandad, whose home allotment filled with delicious edibles inspired me. He taught me that vegetables can be both beautiful and mouthwateringly delicious.

The talented photographer Sam Folan deserves special recognition for capturing the incredible beauty of these plants through his stunning images. Sam's enthusiasm for all things edible undoubtedly enhanced his work, and I hope he utilises that energy in his own allotment.

I also want to acknowledge the kind words and unwavering support from Sophie Allen and everyone at Quadrille. Your encouragement and guidance made this entire process a joy, and I am immensely grateful for the opportunity to work with you as a first-time author.

My family and friends have been my rock throughout this endeavour, helping me transform my back garden into a little piece of paradise known as the Kitchen Garden. We've toiled together, overcoming challenges, and shared countless laughs as we turned a neglected grassy slope into a vibrant and productive space bursting with colour and delicious plants. Mom, thank you for always being there to offer assistance and support, even if you occasionally mistook plants for weeds! Darren, you've been an incredible gardening companion, constantly providing advice, ideas and a continuous source of laughter. I sincerely appreciate your help and friendship. And to my beloved Huspand Matt (yes, spelled just like that), thank you for your unwavering belief in me, your support and encouragement to chase my dreams. I couldn't have come this far or achieved what I have today without you.

Lastly, this book is dedicated to my ever-faithful gardening pooch, Winston. I miss your grumpy face and the way you would explore the garden, 'taste-testing' whatever caught your fancy. But fear not, I know Nipper and Reggie will carry on your legacy with pride.

To everyone who has contributed to this book and my journey, directly or indirectly, I am truly grateful. Your support and assistance have made this endeavour a reality, and I appreciate each and every one of you.

Acknowledgements

◄ Top right:
Winston; Credit:
Darren Lakin;
Bottom left:
Nipper supervising

About the author

Rob Smith is a gardening enthusiast with a lifelong love for the green world. Since childhood, he cherished gardening moments with his grandad, nurturing a fascination for growing food. He now contributes to numerous national gardening magazines and graces TV and radio segments on gardening. Collaborating with multiple horticultural companies, Rob tirelessly searches the globe and seeks out, tests and introduces new vegetable seeds and plants to home gardeners and commercial growers alike. His heart beats for new varieties, while also preserving heritage and heirloom vegetables, breathing life into nearly forgotten delights.

Managing Director Sarah Lavelle
Senior Commissioning Editor Sophie Allen
Designer Alicia House
Photographer Sam Folan
Production Director Stephen Lang
Production Controller Martina Georgieva

Published in 2024 by Quadrille, an imprint of Hardie Grant Publishing

Quadrille
52–54 Southwark Street
London SE1 1UN
quadrille.com

Cataloguing in Publication Data: a catalogue record for this book is available from the British Library.

Text © Rob Smith 2024
Photography © Sam Folan 2024
Design © Quadrille 2024

ISBN 978 1 83783 128 9

Printed in China

MIX
Paper | Supporting responsible forestry
FSC
www.fsc.org
FSC™ C020056